Restitution

Restructuring School Discipline

Facilitator's Guide

Revised Edition

Diane Chelsom Gossen

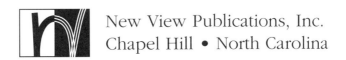
New View Publications, Inc.
Chapel Hill • North Carolina

This book is dedicated to
Judy Anderson

First printing, 1998

RESTITUTION FACILITATOR'S GUIDE, Revised Edition. Copyright © 1998 Diane Chelsom Gossen. All rights reserved. Printed in the United States of America. No part of this book may be used or reproduced in any manner whatsoever without written permission except in the case of brief quotations embodied in critical articles or reviews. For information, address New View Publications, P.O. Box 3021, Chapel Hill, N.C. 27515-3021.

Cover illustration by Ranata Cardin

ISBN 0-944337-37-6

Library of Congress Catalog Card Number 97-075927

Quantity Purchases

Companies, schools, professional groups, clubs, and other organizations may qualify for special terms when ordering quantities of this title. For information contact the Sales Department, New View Publications, P.O. Box 3021, Chapel Hill, N.C., 27515-3021.
1-800-441-3604

CONTENTS

PART 2: TEACHING RESTITUTION

AFTERWORD

APPENDIX: NOTES TO THE FACILITATOR

REFERENCE LIST

INDEX

Introduction

"Teaching kids to count is fine, but teaching them what counts is best."

— *Bob Talbert*

USING THIS GUIDE

The purpose of this guide is to help you implement the Restitution Model in your school. Before doing so, it is important that you have an understanding of Dr. William Glasser's concepts of Control Theory and Quality Schools.

In this guide, I have described the process of learning and applying Restitution in two parts. First, educators must set the stage for less coercive management.* Part I of this guide provides you with materials to help educators evaluate their current management styles and learn new lead-management skills. These skills include self-evaluation, exploring the concept of control, and forming a social contract and setting and maintaining limits with the class. Educators also learn new techniques for managing difficult situations in the classroom. These techniques and skills must be continually and consistently applied in order for the "stage" to be firmly set. Many of the problems that educators encounter when implementing Restitution are a result of not having established a less coercive school environment where these techniques are routinely practiced.

The second part of this guide provides you with materials to teach educators the creative and strengthening process of making a wrong right. They will learn how to help a child frame up, plan, and carry out a restitution. They will also gain a better understanding of how and why this process strengthens children and teaches them self-discipline and responsibility.

In this guide I have provided important discussion points, handouts, and activities which will help you to explore, understand, internalize, and teach the Restitution concepts. I believe that this is an inside-out process. Experiential exercises and constant self-evaluation help us intuitively comprehend the differences between traditional stimulus-response discipline models and the Restitution Model. As the facilitator, you will find these activities invaluable as you help others learn to restructure their discipline practices.

> The activities marked with a star are "inside-out" exercises which are designed to help participants relate these concepts to their own lives and experiences. These activities are valuable because they strengthen self-evaluation skills and cause us to explore these ideas at a personal level. Too often adults evaluate only at the cognitive level, whereas children tend to evaluate at the feeling level. These activities encourage participants to internalize concepts and evaluate at that level.

---

* Non-coercive management is an ideal goal, but not realistic since as human beings we all attempt the impossible—to control each other. I therefore refer to this management style as "less coercive management."

Nothing Happened But Everything Happened

As I've worked with administrators who are implementing Restitution, one of their observations was that teachers and parents were suspicious of the process because children who left the planning session were not chagrined. They did not feel guilty, but instead were energized. They were not dragging their heels. Instead, they were anticipating the task at hand.

To an observer schooled in traditional discipline practices, it appeared that the administrators had not accomplished their job of correcting students. These observers commented, "Nothing happened to the child." At one level, this was valid, for nothing happened *to* the child—but everything happened *within* the child.

Many people lack faith in the self-discipline process if they do not see that something has happened externally to the child. This is due to a belief in the stimulus-response concept that it is the adults' job to motivate and control the child *from without*. Conversely, the process of Restitution is grounded in the belief of internal motivation and self-change. We believe that people *intrinsically* want to do well, to get along with other people, and to make reparations for their wrongs. Restitution focuses on children's internal motivation to fix their mistakes and to become better people. As a result of a value shift at the higher level, new behaviors are learned that can be used in other situations. When we see a child become strengthened, more positive, and energized, then we know the process is working.

Restitution, as outlined in this guide, is a growth process for everyone involved—adults as well as children. Helping a child create a restitution is a much more fulfilling experience than acting as monitor or punisher. As educators, implementing the Restitution Model is really about helping children learn to become better people. We create the conditions for a child to lift himself out of failure and to leave behind blame and denial. The child is strengthened and his self-understanding can be used to help other children—and so the positive cycle continues.

Philosophical Tenets

Restitution is based on the following philosophical tenets:

- Mistakes are normal; to err is human.

- People know when they have done something wrong.

- Guilt and criticism contribute to defensive behavior. When under attack, people put up walls and use a lot of energy rationalizing past wrongs to preserve their self-esteem.

- If people see themselves as successful, they will be more open to learning a better way to behave. If we view them as capable, responsible, and willing to change, even in the face of their mistakes, they have an incentive to move forward.

- The process of making a restitution strengthens people. One of the most important skills in life is learning to repair our own mistakes.

- People won't lie or hide their mistakes if they believe they are capable of making restitution and will be given an opportunity to do so.

- The process of making a restitution is a creative one which builds problem-solving skills in the offender.

- People who are given the opportunity to make a restitution are generous with others who make mistakes. As parents and teachers, they tend not to be punitive with their own children.

In order to practice Restitution we need to have a deep understanding of the following:

- We have no desire to hurt children because abuse only perpetuates a cycle of violence.

- We believe in strengthening the child who offends so he will have less desire to hurt others.

- We believe that rewards disrupt a child's internal locus of control. When a child's locus of control is external, he behaves to please others rather than to self-actualize and become the best person he can be.

- We believe that children can understand and share our commitment to caring and cooperation.

- We believe that telling people they are wrong does not help them do right.

- We believe children can learn a better way to behave.

Exit Outcomes	Restitution
Acquire, integrate, and use knowledge at all levels	Planning a restitution involves higher level thinking skills, including application, analysis, and synthesis. Restitution is a creative art and a right-brain activity.
Acquire and use process skills: • group dynamics • problem-solving • communication • conflict resolution • decision-making	Restitution is a collaborative problem-solving process which focuses on making things right and resolving conflicts. Restitution sets the stage for learning: • It's OK to make a mistake. Learning begins when things don't work right. • Learning how to focus on solutions is an important life skill.
Maintain self-esteem	Restitution is first and foremost about strengthening the offender—helping her to become the kind of person she wants to be. It does not focus solely on the victim. In planning a restitution the child controls her own behavior. This satisfies her power need. Restitution stabilizes the child's success identity. Restitution enables the child to reclaim self-esteem through personal effort.
Show concern and respect for others.	Restitution is the action of making a full reparation. In making a restitution, the child refers to the social contract, which includes the beliefs and values about how we treat others. Restitution strengthens relationships.
Be a self-directed, lifelong learner.	The goal of Restitution is self-discipline. Restitution helps children evaluate what they can do to fix their own mistakes. Restitution strengthens a child's internal locus of control.

Part I

Setting the Stage for Less Coercive Management

"At every step the child should be allowed to
meet the real experiences of life; the thorns
should never be plucked from the roses."

— *Ellen Key*

Learning a New Mental Model

1. THE ILLUSIONS OF CONTROL

GOAL

▶ To explore and discuss illusions of control

REFERENCE

▶ *Restitution,* pages 1-22

FACILITATOR'S NOTES

▶ Chapter One of *Restitution* deals with four illusions of control. In order for teachers to become Managers, they must discard several common, deeply ingrained misconceptions. Discuss the following illusions with workshop participants. Ask them whether they share any of these "illusions." Are they willing to reevaluate their beliefs about control?

1. *The illusion that we control the student.*
   We can't force anyone to do something he doesn't choose to do. Even when it appears we are controlling a student's behavior, he is allowing us to control him; at the moment it is his most need-fulfilling choice. Control Theory tells us that all behavior is purposeful, even behavior we don't like.

2. *The illusion that all positive reinforcement works and is beneficial.*
   Positive reinforcement or persuasion is controlling. Any attempt to influence a student to repeat a behavior is an attempt to control him. After awhile the student begins to recognize this and resists our attempts, or he may become dependent on the teacher's opinion of his efforts.

3. *The illusion that criticism and guilt build character.*
   Using criticism and guilt to control children leads to their development of a failure identity. They learn to feel badly about themselves. They develop negative self-talk. Sometimes it is hard for teachers to recognize that they use these behaviors, because often it is only their tone of voice that conveys the negative message.

4. *The illusion that adults have the right to coerce.*
   Many adults believe that they have the responsibility to make children do certain things. Whatever it takes is accceptable if it results in measurable performance improvement. By the time that adults realize that coercive behaviors are ineffective in the long run, an adversarial relationship usually already exists.

2. SHIFTING OUR MENTAL MODELS

GOAL

▶ To learn a new mental model of discipline

REFERENCE

▶ *Restitution,* pages ix-xv

FACILITATOR'S NOTES

▶ Discuss the following with workshop participants:

- The "Illusions of Control" represent "mental models." Peter Senge in *The Fifth Discipline* defines mental models as "deeply ingrained assumptions, generalizations, or even pictures or images that influence how we understand the world and how we take action."

- These "illusions" or mental models are open to challenge. Each assumption—no matter how firmly held—is open to challenge at the experiential and intellectual level. The challenge of Restitution is that it invites us to re-examine our basic beliefs in how we deal with others.

- The challenges of Restitution are: (1) to shift your mental model about human behavior; (2) to shift your discipline paradigm.

- How does one make a shift from a stimulus-response perspective to a Control Theory approach? Stephen R. Covey in *Principle-Centered Leadership* says that "if you want to make slow, incremental improvement, change your attitude or behavior." However, he emphasizes that if you want to improve in major ways you also need to change your frame of reference. "Change how you see the world, how you think about people....Change your paradigm, your scheme for understanding and explaining certain aspects of reality."

- The chart on the opposite page outlines the differences between the stimulus-response view of the world and the Control Theory view of the world.

- Senge warns that the difficulty with changing mental models is that they usually exist below the level of awareness. "Very often, we are not consciously aware of our mental models or the effects they have on our behavior." If we remain unaware of our mental models, they remain unexamined and, therefore, unchanged.

Stimulus-Response View of the World	Control-Theory View of the World
Our realities are the same	Our realities are separate
Everybody sees the same pictures	Everybody has different pictures
We try to convert people to our view of the world	We try to understand the other person's view of the world
Misbehavior is seen as a mistake	All behavior is seen as purposeful
Others can control me	You can only control yourself
I can control others	You can't control others
Coercion is practiced when persuasion fails	Collaboration and consensus create new options
Win/lose mental model	Win/win mental model

- •. In managing mental models at the personal level, Senge talks about the importance of asking yourself what you believe about the way the world works. Then ask yourself, "Am I willing to consider that this generalization may be inaccurate or misleading?" The second question is important because, if the answer is no, there is no point in proceeding.

- • Peter Senge recognizes that the "inertia of deeply entrenched mental models can overwhelm even the best systemic insights….The discipline of working with mental models starts with turning the mirror inward; learning to unearth our internal pictures of the world, to bring them to the surface and hold them rigorously to scrutiny."

- • As educators, we need to turn the mirror inward and look at our internal pictures of what we believe about children. Each of us needs to examine our own discipline practices. Do we harbor the illusion that we can make others conform? Do we believe it is our responsibility to coerce? Or do we accept that each individual has the right to free choice providing he doesn't interfere with others meeting their needs? I have been using Control Theory ideas for two decades and still, to this day, hear myself posing questions that are controlling (rather than sincere requests to elicit information). Awareness is the first step toward a paradigm shift.

- When working with the illusions of control, the facilitator must remember that each of these illusions represents a "mental model" that is strongly held by our culture. For example, the stimulus-response mental model tells us that other people can make us happy, angry, or sad and that our behavior is a response to their actions. Many of our child-rearing methods are then predicated upon ways to control young people so that they don't control us. There are treatises written on techniques of motivation and reinforcement because we believe that this is the job of adults in our society. It is not easy to reorient educators and ask them to give up the belief in external motivation in favor of internal motivation.

- This task is almost impossible without learning Control Theory. I learned Control Theory from Dr. William Glasser who learned it from William Powers. It took me six months before I cognitively grasped the ideas and two years before I was able to grasp them viscerally and teach them well.

- In his book *Control Theory*, Glasser explains, "We are not controlled by external events, difficult as they may be. We are motivated completely by forces inside ourselves, and all of our behavior is our attempt to control our own lives." Implementing the concepts of Control Theory and Restitution—very different mental models from those of stimulus-response—will not happen instantly. This process is gradual and begins with a strong knowledge base.

3. MANAGEMENT STYLES

GOALS

▶ To understand the five positions of control

▶ To self-evaluate your own management style in terms of the five positions of control

REFERENCE

▶ *Restitution,* pages 1-3, 28-40

HANDOUTS

▶ Five Positions of Control (page 16)

▶ Who Would Say...? (page 17)

▶ Where Are You? (page 18)

▶ Shifting From Monitor to Manager (page 19)

FACILITATOR'S NOTES

▶ Put numbers 1-5 on the floor representing the five positions of control. Stand by each number as you role play the corresponding management style. Spend 2-3 minutes role playing each position of control with a volunteer:

1. *Punisher:* [point finger, angry voice] "You're always late and never on time! I can't count on you for anything. You're hopeless!"

2. *Guilter:* [soft, guilting voice] "I can't believe you're late. I was worried about you. I'm so disappointed. I thought I could count on you."

3. *Buddy:* [friendly voice, compliments, joking manner] "Hey, you're a little late. You're such a fast runner. Next time be punctual so we can have more time together. You'll do it for me—won't you?"

4. *Monitor:* [even tone] "What's the rule? What's the consequence for being late? Go to detention. Can you do that? Thank you."

5. *Manager:* [sincere tone] "It's OK to make a mistake. Do you want to make it right? Are you the kind of person who wants to fix a mistake? What could you do? What do you want to give back? What do we believe about this?"

▶ Identify for participants the key aspects of each position of control:

1. *Punisher:* Points at child and scolds. "Always" and "never" are common words. The child takes the Punisher out of his quality world. The result is usually rebellion.

2. *Guilter:* Is more hurtful than the Punisher. The Guilter stays in the child's quality world. Guilt results in poor self-concept as the punished child thinks he is a bad person.

3. *Buddy:* Focus is on the positive. The child does things for the Buddy not for himself and dependency results.

4. *Monitor:* Asks "What's the rule?" and "What's the consequence?" The consequence discomforts the child, and reinforcement works only while the monitor is watching.

5. *Manager:* Focuses on values and beliefs of the child; asks, "Do you think it's important that…?"; or, "Are you the kind of person that wants to fix a mistake?"; lets the child figure out how to remedy the situation.

▶ Discuss each management style using the handout "Five Positions of Control" on page 16. Emphasize the effectiveness of each position in building strength and responsibility in our children.

ACTIVITIES

▶ **Who Would Say…?**
Have participants work with a partner or in a small group. Think about who would say the statements on the handout "Who Would Say…?" on page 17.

▶ **Where Are You?** ☆
Use the handout "Where Are You?" on page 18. Ask the participants to evaluate their own management styles at school and at home. Then they should place themselves on the continuum from Punisher to Manager. After the activity, encourage people to share what they have learned about themselves.

▶ **Role Play: Five Positions of Control**
Think of an example of an inappropriate behavior and role play the five positions of control with your workshop participants. Remember to change your nonverbal messages and your tone of voice as you demonstrate the different positions of control.

Example: A seventeen-year-old hits a curb while driving your car, and now the alignment is bad.

1. *Punisher:* "I'm furious with you! You're grounded for the rest of your life."

2. *Guilter:* "Didn't I warn you? You could have killed yourself. I'm so disappointed!"

3. *Buddy:* "Don't worry, I'll pay for it."

4. *Monitor:* "I'll have to do this to you. You can't use the car."

5. *Manager:* "What's the plan to fix it?"

▶ **Identify Positions of Control**

Have the group identify examples of each position of control in the story "Snowballs" on pages 52-56 in *Restitution*. Below is the answer key:

1. *Punishment:* "I resisted the temptation to shove him…" [Author felt like punishing.]

2. *Guilt:* "He heaved a sigh of relief…" [Why? Author had guilt in her voice or Jake was choosing to feel guilty.]

3. *Buddy:* "I have confidence you can work this out…if you need my input, come and ask." [Author gives support.]

4. *Monitor:* "Just don't give us the ten dollars." [The boys impose a consequence on themselves.]

5. *Manager:* "Three hours later they returned triumphant…." [The boys carry out a restitution successfully.]

▶ **Shifting From Monitor To Manager**

Have a group discussion outlining the differences between a Monitor and a Manager. You may want to refer to the handout "Shifting From Monitor To Manager" on page 19.

FAILURE IDENTITY		SUCCESS IDENTITY		
Punisher	*Guilter*	*Buddy*	*Monitor*	*Manager*
Negative Controlling Behaviors		Positive Controlling Behaviors		Self-Control
Knows the punishment	Internalizes the punishment and feels like a bad person	Feels his fortune is dependent on the adult doing things for him	Understands he has transgressed and earned a negative consequence	Understands he is responsible to make amends to another
Child takes the punisher out of his quality world	Child keeps the punisher in his quality world	Adult is very important person in his quality world	Child puts picture of society's laws in his quality world	Child puts picture of himself as capable in his quality world
• Criticizing • Threatening • Hurting • Sarcasm • Isolating	• Sighing • Moralizing • Personalizing • Silencing • Disappointing	• Joking • Teasing • Complimenting • Encouraging • Overextending	• Reinforcing • Reasoning • Measuring • Fining • Grounding	• Questioning • Guiding • Brainstorming • Assessing

Who Would Say?

Work with a partner or in a small group. Think about who would say the following questions and statements.

PUNISHER

GUILTER

BUDDY

MONITOR

MANAGER

1. I'm disappointed in you. .... _____

2. You never get it right. .... _____

3. Do it for me. .... _____

4. Do you want a happy-face sticker today? .... _____

5. Didn't you say you'd do it? .... _____

6. You're always the last one to finish. .... _____

7. How can you make it better? .... _____

8. You won't get a star if you don't finish. .... _____

9. How many times have I told you? .... _____

10. Remember what I did for you? .... _____

11. You'll never get anywhere in life. .... _____

12. What's your plan to fix it? .... _____

Mark yourself on the continuum by putting an "X" on the line.

1	**2**	**3**	**4**	**5**
Punisher	**Guilter**	**Buddy**	**Monitor**	**Manager**

_____

(At Home)

_____

(At School)

When I was a new teacher, I behaved like my own sixth-grade teacher. I was punitive and said things like "No laughing." I would evaluate my management style at that time as follows:

—————————**X**—————————————————————

Now evaluate your own management style at a particular stage of your life. Put an "X" on the line below and indicate what this stage was. Discuss how and why you've changed.

_____

MONITOR	MANAGER
Provides minimal choices	Provides many choices
Outcome known from the start	Outcome unknown at start
Teacher-directed	Child-driven
States what will happen	Asks questions
External motivation	Internal motivation
Teacher evaluation	Self-evaluation
Teaches external control	Teaches self-control
Does not help meet child's four, basic psychological needs	Helps child meet all four basic psychological needs

Moving Toward Self-Discipline

4. CLASSROOM MANAGEMENT TECHNIQUES

GOAL

▶ To understand the conditions which lead to self-discipline

REFERENCE

▶ *Restitution*, pages 65-104

HANDOUT

▶ The Least-Coercive Road (page 24)

FACILITATOR'S NOTES

▶ Building a less coercive classroom environment, where self-discipline and Restitution can occur, requires a progression of learning and applying management techniques.

▶ In this section of the facilitator's guide, various classroom techniques are organized around these three steps:

1. *Opening Up The Territory* ("Does It Really Matter?," "Yes, If…")

2. *Gaining Consent: The Social Contract* ("Build a Common Picture," "Discuss Common Values and Beliefs")

3. *Setting and Maintaining Limits* ("What's the Rule?," "My Job Is…, Your Job Is…")

Also, see the handout on page 24 for a diagram that illustrates the steps which set the stage for Restitution.

▶ **Stage 1: Opening Up the Territory**
We can only control ourselves, it is not possible to control another human being. This Control Theory concept is new to many people and accepting it opens up the territory for changing how we work with our students. It is futile to control another, yet we continuously, creatively, and sometimes even deviously attempt to do so. When another person attempts to control us, we experience frustration and sense a loss of freedom. Therefore, the most desirable arrangement between two human beings is when options are maximized and control over the other is minimized. Traditionally, schools have tended to do the opposite—reduce options and increase control. This trend has stunted the learning process as students' energies have been spent resisting control and teachers' energies have been spent attempting to accept limited options

rather than freeing students to create new options for themselves. Opening up the territory increases options for both teachers and students. The goal of this stage is to build freedom and choices into the process. This can be gradually undertaken so that students faced with a new sense of freedom do not take unfair advantage of their teachers. The goals of Stage I are to:

- Recognize that you can only control yourself. This can be accomplished by using one of the coercion exercises (pages 26-27).

- Become aware of each time you attempt to control another. Awareness precedes change. This awareness can be gained through the exercise "Does It Really Matter?" (pages 27-28).

- Self-evaluate. What do we value highly enough to deny another person's request? Is it possible to figure out a way to acquiesce and still meet our own needs? The exercise "Yes, If..." (pages 28-30) illustrates how to do this.

Understanding the implications of interfering with another's freedom can have a powerful effect on the relationship between any two human beings. The practice of opening up the territory in a relationship helps meet each individual's need for freedom and it sets the stage for developing a social contract.

▶ Stage 2: The Social Contract

The social contract is the covenant by which individuals decide to share a common path. Carl Glickman, author of *Renewing American Schools,* says this can only be achieved by moving from a congenial to a collegial culture in the school. A collegial culture can be recognized by the willingness of the members to discuss and explore what they believe at a deep level. They are not afraid to share their ideas and differences of opinion. To better understand the importance of shared beliefs, it is helpful to read William Power's *Behavior: The Control of Perception* or Ed Ford's *Freedom From Stress.* Both of these books discuss the systems concept at the highest level of perception. William Powers says, "I count belief and unbelief together as a systems concept. There is nothing inherently wrong with either—if there were we would not have evolved with the capacity to form beliefs or unbeliefs. What goes wrong at this level of organization is loss of the ability to alter the organization of one's belief systems to achieve harmony among all the different belief systems necessary to complete life—different belief systems inside oneself and different belief systems among different people." In order to establish a social contract about what we want and how we will operate as a group, it is necessary to have an overlapping system of beliefs (and "unbeliefs") among a group of people. In order to establish a social contract at classroom, school, and district levels, people must:

- Be aware of their own picture album.
- Have the picture of working with other people in their albums.
- Be open to sharing their own pictures as well as listening to others share theirs.

- Find common ground.
- Decide to work together towards common pictures.

▶ Stage 3: Setting and Maintaining Limits

Whereas Stage I deals with our innate desire and need for freedom and Stage II deals with man's desire to bond with others, to actualize his higher self, and to live according to his beliefs, Stage III deals with power. Once a social contract has been established, those agreeing to it then need to uphold it. This includes spelling out roles and rules. The group has the right to set limitations on members who fail to honor their obligations. In a school setting, after we have established our goals and exit outcomes, the group decides the roles and duties of each member. Rules are also established by the group. They then decide on sanctions or consequences and who will enforce them. In the classroom, the teacher is usually the enforcer although a group of children may have a role in the process. Once these rules and limitations are established, each member of the group chooses either to manage himself or herself toward the common goal or break the covenant and leave the group.

▶ Summary, Stages 1-3

Each of these stages is important when establishing a less coercive environment. To help children we need to give them choices and establish positive, common pictures based on universal beliefs. When we ask children, "What is the rule?" we focus on the limits we have established as a group.

▶ Stage 4: Moving to Restitution

Although the group can sanction an individual, it is better to help him create a restitution which is tied to his beliefs. When we ask, "What do we believe?" we move to a higher plane—to our values as established in the social contract. If the child has been a legitimate participant in forming the social covenant, we can discuss how we respect others. Control Theory psychology teaches us to build upon the foundation of the social contract through positive involvement and win-win solutions.

Coercion Exercises
Does It Really Matter?
Yes, If…

Beliefs
Values
Our Ideal Classroom

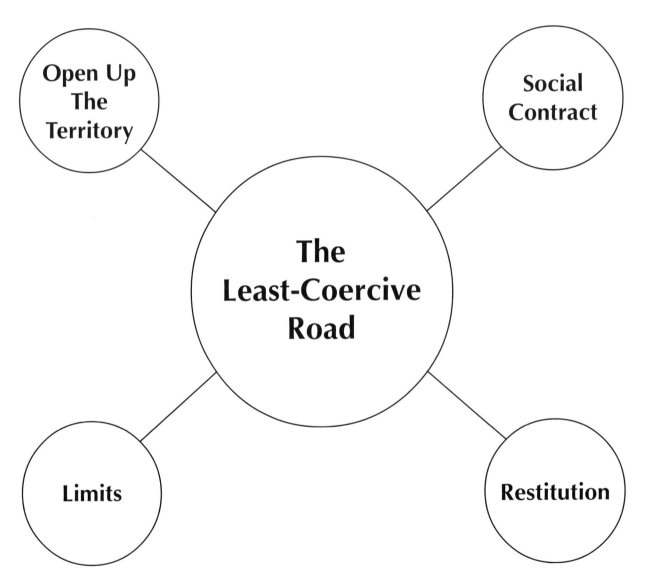

What's the rule?
Roles (My Job Is…, My Job Is Not…)
Words, 10%/Tone, 35%/Non-Verbal, 55%

Characteristics
Locators: Belief, Category, & Time
Restitution Triangle

5. OPENING UP THE TERRITORY

GOALS

▶ To understand classroom management techniques for reducing the number of interventions

▶ To better meet both the teacher's and the students' need for freedom by increasing options

REFERENCE

▶ *Restitution,* pages 65-70

HANDOUTS

▶ Does It Really Matter? (page 31)

▶ Yes, If… (page 32)

FACILITATOR'S NOTES

▶ Coercion Exercises: The first step in the process is for educators to understand that we can only control ourselves. Attempting to get others to do what we want when they have no intention of doing so is a waste of our time and energy. On pages 26-27 there are two exercises that illustrate the futility of coercive behaviors. These exercises have the same theme, but vary in the times they take to complete.

▶ Once educators make the mind shift from external to internal motivation, they can learn new techniques to reduce the number of interventions, thus "opening up the territory." Opening up the territory gives the child more freedom, which is necessary for the child to develop responsibility. Children develop responsibility by exploring options and learning from their own decisions. Therefore, space between the teacher and the student is essential.

▶ Opening up the territory is not a laissez-faire, permissive approach. The teacher and students decide which beliefs are important in terms of goals in the classroom, and then they focus on actualizing these principles. As the teacher intervenes less, the students gain freedom so that they are more willing to listen when she talks about what is really important—values and learning. The teacher learns a better way to meet her need for freedom because there is less monitoring of nonessential things. Two activities that deal with the concept of shifting from a negative to a positive focus are: "Does It Really Matter?" (pages 27-28) and "Yes, If…" (pages 28-30).

ACTIVITIES

▶ **Coercion Exercise Number 1: Closed Fist** ☆

Time: 10 minutes. The purpose of this activity is to discover the variety of strategies each of us uses to influence other people, to evaluate these strategies, and to understand that no strategy can be guaranteed to motivate others if they choose non-compliance.

Ask the participants to divide into pairs.

1. One partner will be called **A** and the other partner, **B**.

2. Ask the **A**'s to clench their fists. Then say, "Now **B**'s, get **A**'s to open their fists."

3. Observe the strategies that **B**'s use to accomplish this task. There will be a variety of techniques (both positive and negative) used by **B** in an attempt to influence **A** to comply.

4. Process the activity as a large group. Ask participants to identify the strategies, and make a list. Possible strategies include:

Bribery	Being a buddy	Bargaining
Voice Control	Violence	Abuse
Reasoning	Questioning	Guilt
Trickery	Diversion	Logic
Asking	Sweet-talking	Compliments
Touching	Crying	

5. Discuss the large amount of time and the various ways that we try to control each other. We all use a wide variety of behaviors—some positive and some negative—to do this. This exercise provides a good opportunity to have fun and laugh at ourselves. It also helps participants understand that we all have a choice whether we will allow others to control us or not.

This exercise was taught to me by Suzy Hallock.

▶ **Coercion Exercise Number 2: You Got It, I Want It** ☆

Time: 20 minutes. The purpose of this activity is to illustrate the coercive behaviors we all use to try to get what we want.

Divide the participants into pairs. If possible, include a man and a woman in each pair.

1. Label one partner A and one partner B. A has something B wants. You determine

what that "something" is (for example: jewelry, a jacket, a ride home, or a switched shift at work).

2. B has to try to get A to give him or her the desired item. B should try several different behaviors to persuade A. These may include reasoning, begging, conning, or threatening.

3. A's job is to resist, to say no, or "It's not my job (my responsibility, my obligation, etc.)."

4. These exchanges should continue for about two minutes. As the trainer, you may encourage them to "try harder."

5. After two minutes, call "time" and instruct the participants to talk with each other about their experiences.

   • Which was the hardest emotion to deal with?

   • What did you do to defend yourself that worked?

   • How many people got what they wanted?

6. Reverse the roles and repeat the activity.

7. Once both partners have played both roles, discuss the following points as a large group:

   • We probably dislike many of these coercive behaviors even though we find that we sometimes resort to using them ourselves.

   • Some of these behaviors are more controlling than others.

   • We can only be controlled if we choose or allow ourselves to be controlled.

This exercise was taught to me by Barnes Boffey, Ed.D.

▶ **Does It Really Matter** ☆
The three goals for this activity are: to identify areas in which we try to control other people; to select and prioritize the standards which reflect our values; to identify the beliefs behind the limitations we want to set on others.

1. Introduce "Does It Really Matter?" by using a wide variety of personal examples.

   • Does it really matter if a child wears matching socks? Isn't it more important that the child is warm and clean?

   • Does it really matter if the towels are folded in two or three folds? Do the towels know the difference?

   • Does it really matter who wins a game of tennis between friends?

Use as much humor as possible and create your own examples. As an illustration, I tell the story of helping someone load a dishwasher in the kitchen only to hear them reloading it when I go to the living room. Does it really matter? Do the cups know the difference?

2. Stress the importance of asking "Does it really matter?" This question gives freedom both to the follower and the leader. The follower gains options to do things in their own way. The leaders gain freedom from responsibility—it takes an enormous amount of energy to monitor people all the time. The leader is "tight" on what they believe and "loose" on how it is accomplished. This strengthens the "loose-tight" connection.

3. Activity Guidelines:

   - Have participants discuss the handout "Does It Really Matter?" on page 31. Our positive experiences with people in the form of shared time, jokes, and unconditional statements are like deposits in the emotional bank. They build up our collateral with these people. Every time we say, "Don't do it that way, do it my way instead," we make a withdrawal and we lose some of our collateral. A major withdrawal is a request that does really matter. Examples include: requests related to safety, confidentiality, shared work responsibility, and respect. Those we supervise are more likely to discuss values with us if we are not always attempting to control them. For example, my teenager is more likely to listen to me talk about safe driving when I have not already commented on his messy hair, his ripped jeans, or his suede shoes that he wore in the snow.

   - Emphasize that people have the right to set their own standards. The leader should not pass judgment on these standards unless they involve irresponsibly hurting another person.

   - Ask participants to evaluate whether the standards they have chosen are getting them what they want in their relationships. We need to ask ourselves whether it really matters every time we have the urge to control someone else.

   - As participants review these questions, point out that in a given set of circumstances the answer to any one of the questions on the sheet could be yes. The teacher's reply to a child is based on the context of the situation. The teacher is encouraged to have an internal dialogue before she attempts to control the child, in order to be sure it is worth the effort.

▶ **Yes, If…** ☆

Have participants discuss the handout "Yes, If…" on page 32. The goal of this activity is to increase the number of positive answers given to student requests. In order to get into a person's quality world they need to hear yes more often than no. Two ways to get into people's quality worlds are:

- Tie what we have to say to the pictures that are already in their quality worlds.
- Say yes to what they want, providing it doesn't interfere with what we want.

Note: Saying yes does not mean capitulating at one's own expense. Say yes if you get what you need, if I get what I need, or if the system gets what it needs.

The "if" in "Yes, if…" is always related to what I need. If I feel like saying no, it is an indication to me that the person is asking for something which I perceive as a violation of my needs. I must ask myself, "What need do I think is threatened?" By answering that question, I can generate the "Yes, if…" For example, if my secretary wants two days off, and I feel like saying no, I would ask myself this question. I want to say no because I have a speech to be typed. Once I recognize this, I can convert the no to a yes. I can say "Yes, if you can type this speech before you leave." This retort would be more honest and effective than saying, "You have already used up your vacation days this month," or, "No, because it's not in our agreement."

Discuss three possible misconceptions when saying "Yes, if…"

1. *Choosing an "if" which is not achievable.*
   For example, a principal once said to me, "The 'yes if' works so well at school, I decided to use it at home. The problem was, after two days, my seven-year-old said to me, 'Don't say "Yes, if…" Daddy.' This mystified me." I said to the principal, "What did you say after the 'yes, if,' Dave? Was what you asked your son to do possible?" He giggled. We discovered that what he had been asking the child to do was something beyond the child's ability. In the initial stages of applying a "Yes, if…" strategy be sure the conditions are simple and achievable so the child is motivated to engage in problem-solving. After a child is accustomed to "Yes, if…" management, he will be able to solve multifaceted problems on his own because he has already had success with the process. My seventeen-year-old can now find solutions to the problems which stymie me.

2. *Taking unfair advantage of an important request.*
   This can occur when people under our authority make a request and we sense it is something they really want. Our eyes light up as possibilities for extortion present themselves. Because these people are candid enough to reveal the desire, we have the opportunity to exploit them. For example, my son asks if he may go to a rock concert. I know this is important to him. I say, "Yes, if your room is cleaned up…if you get a hair cut…if you write a letter to your grandparents." None of the preceding conditions have anything to do with my need to say no to his request. I have failed to apply the "Yes, if…" formula to myself: "What is my need to say no?" The answers are, "It's too expensive. Driving could be dangerous. You won't get up for school the next morning." The answers to my son are: "Yes, if you have the money. Yes, if there's a responsible driver. Yes, if you can get yourself up for school the next morning." These replies are authentic and

nonexploitive. Unlike the previous responses, they are not designed to disrupt him getting what he wants in order to get what I want from him.

3. *Saying yes to all requests.*
   Sometimes there are policies that require a manager to say no. This does not mean that this manager is a boss-manager; it means that in this particular situation the manager does not have the resources to work toward a positive answer. He is not a boss-manager if he generally tries to say yes as often as possible.

Does it really matter…

- If he sits with his feet on the floor?

- If she chews gum or not?

- If they are silent while working?

- If she pays attention?

- If he does his homework?

- If she fails an exam?

- If they want to change seats?

- If he participates in an extracurricular activity?

- If she writes neatly?

- If he understands the lesson?

- If she participates in a class discussion?

- If he wears an earring?

- If he shows up on time?

- If she has a clean desk?

- If he hands in an assignment late?

- If she puts her hand up before talking?

What reason would you give the child for requiring his or her compliance for each of the above issues?

This activity requires adults to identify and evaluate requests from children to which they normally answer no or "No, because . . ." The requests are usually simple ones such as "May I sharpen my pencil?" The answer may be "No, because I'm talking." However, a better answer would be one which redirects the child, such as "Yes, when I'm finished giving instructions."

In order to increase the number of positive replies:

- Say yes as often as you can.

- If you can't say yes, say "Yes, if…" or "Yes, when…" and add the necessary condition.

- When you say no, give the child your reason and don't change your mind.

Educators and parents have a lot of fun doing this activity! First work in small groups of four or five. Create your own examples based on your experiences. Then choose an example to share with the whole group. Examples:

May we have a dance?	✗	No, because I said so.
	✓	Yes, if we can have a month to plan it.
May we listen to the radio?	✗	No, because it would be too distracting.
	✓	Yes, if everyone stays on task.
May I go to the bathroom?	✗	No, because then everyone will want to go.
	✓	Yes, if you wait until I've finished my instruction and only one person goes at a time.

6. GAINING CONSENT: THE SOCIAL CONTRACT

GOALS

▶ To understand the importance in reaching a consensus with students on a common picture of the ideal classroom and a common set of beliefs and values

▶ To understand that establishing a social contract is an essential prerequisite for effectively implementing Restitution

REFERENCE

▶ *Restitution*, pages 71-73

HANDOUTS

▶ Mission and Rules (page 35)

▶ Find the Belief (pages 36-37)

FACILITATOR'S NOTES

▶ Establishing a common picture and a common set of beliefs and values is essential in setting the stage for Restitution.

▶ Teachers can use several procedures with their students to build a common picture of how they will work together in the classroom.

▶ This process involves a discussion with the students about the ideal classroom picture and the values they want to hold as a group. The emphasis on values reminds the students not only of their rights but also of their obligations to the social contract.

▶ These values and beliefs always relate back to the district and school mission statement and exit outcomes.

▶ Asking the following questions helps students focus on their ideal classroom pictures.

- What do you want?
- What do you need?
- How would you like it to be?

▶ Restitution is primarily about gaining self-balance. Each of us has pictures of the way we want things to be. The higher level pictures reflect the values we hold. These pictures are like mental magnets; they draw us toward using behaviors which match what is important to us. When we perceive ourselves to be out of balance with the way we want to be, we are uncomfortable and seek to restore ourselves back to the people we picture ourselves to be.

▶ When helping a student plan a restitution, refer back to the social contract. The answers to the following questions help students regain balance:

- "What do we/you believe?"
- "What is our/your picture of the ideal classroom?"
- "What are the common values we agreed on as a class?"
- "What kind of a person do you want to be?"

▶ The rules in the classroom flow from the common values and beliefs established in the social contract. Once the social contract is in place, these rules can be established. When students ask about the necessity of a rule, the teacher should remind students of what they agreed upon in the social contract. Discuss the handout "Mission and Rules" on page 35.

ACTIVITIES

▶ Family Beliefs and Values ☆
This activity allows participants an opportunity to reflect on and embrace the differences and similarities among families. Ask participants to divide into small groups and identify a common set of family beliefs. Have the small groups share their lists with the entire group and write them on a blackboard or flip chart. Then give the small groups the task of deriving a list of beliefs for the school. After a few minutes a group member will probably indicate that the list being developed is very similar to the list of the family beliefs.

▶ Classroom Beliefs and Values ☆
In small groups, ask participants to identify a set of values and beliefs for their classrooms. Also discuss the process they might use with students to reach a consensus on a common picture of the ideal classroom and a common set of beliefs and values. After the small group discussions, process as a large group.

▶ Find the Belief ☆
Using the two-page handout "Find the Belief" on pages 36-37, discuss the philosophical issues on the first page. With a partner or in a small group, ask participants to identify the belief associated with each rule on the second page. Process as a large group. Ask these questions:

- Does it really matter?
- How important are these rules?
- Can you still hold the belief without enforcing the rule?

Mission:

To create and promote…

- A warm, safe, caring environment

- Self-esteem—emotional, social, physical, intellectual—through an appreciation of uniqueness, diversity, and individuality

- Successful, challenging, motivating, meaningful, and lifelong learning

- A sense of belonging to family and community

- Fun and celebration

- Honor—respect for self and others—citizenship—cooperation

- Choices, responsibility, problem-solving, decision-making

- Communication

- Aesthetic appreciation

Rules:

- We honor ourselves, others, and the environment.

- I am responsible for myself, my choices, and my actions.

This statement of mission was developed by the students and staff at Tumwater Hill Elementary School

What Do We Believe? (Family)

1. Treat each other with respect and consideration (Ask: What is your picture of respect?)

2. Each has duties and chores (carries own weight).

3. Each person is a unique individual.

4. Each has the right to be safe and secure.

5. We honor confidentiality.

6. Spiritual development is important.

7. We make choices responsibly.

8. We love you unconditionally.

9. Both work and play is important.

10. We share our thoughts, time, and things.

Philosophical Issues

Do you believe that...

1. People have an innate desire to learn?

2. People are intrinsically good?

3. People want to help each other?

4. You can't control another?

5. All behavior is purposeful?

6. We create our own realities?

7. If nothing is risked, nothing is gained?

Developed by staff of Quesnel School District, British Columbia

Find the Belief, Part 2

Discuss what we believe in the work place. Then identify the beliefs which we associate with the following rules. You may add your own rules to the list.

RULE	BELIEF
Make your bed.	
Rinse and put your glass in the dishwasher or sink.	
Arrive at school 30 minutes before classes begin.	
Don't wear blue jeans to work.	
A basic course must be taken before an advanced course.	
Line up to get in the building.	
Don't wear hats to school.	
Fill in a time sheet.	
Don't make fun of someone.	
There must be a designated authority in the workplace at all times.	
Stay on task.	
Meet the deadline.	
Take turns.	

7. Setting And Maintaining Limits

GOALS

▶ To understand classroom management techniques for setting and maintaining limits

▶ To understand a process for defining the role of the teacher and student

▶ To understand the guidelines for rule-making

▶ To apply techniques in avoiding confrontation

▶ To evaluate your own classroom rules

REFERENCE

▶ *Restitution*, pages 7-8 and 73-78

HANDOUTS

▶ What's Your Job? (page 41)

▶ My Job Is… [Sample] (page 42)

▶ My Job Is… (page 43)

▶ Classroom Rules (page 44)

▶ Maintaining Limits (page 45)

▶ Rules for Rules (page 46)

▶ What's the Rule? (page 47)

FACILITATOR'S NOTES

▶ Setting limits revolves around the students doing their job and the teacher doing his or her job—which is to help the *students* do their job. When developed by the teacher and the students together, defining the roles in the classroom gives direction. It also leads to discussions of unrealistic expectations of the teacher or the students. This helps students understand and define the limits to these roles.

▶ The concept of coercion should be explored in depth with the students. Refer to pages 7-8 of *Restitution* for an example of such a classroom discussion. Basically, I tell students that I refuse to put coercion in my job description because I don't believe I can meet a commitment to make anyone do anything. It is not my job. My job is to offer information, to offer examples, to answer questions, to demonstrate, to explore, to question. It is the students' job to learn if they decide it is what they want.

▶ Setting limits flows from the social contract (see previous section on "Gaining Consent—The Social Contract"). Once students have discussed the ideal classroom picture and the values they want to hold as a group, they negotiate roles, rules, and consequences. The purpose of this section is to learn how to define these in the classroom.

▶ There are several classroom management techniques and questions that teachers can use to set and maintain the limits.

- Negotiate rules and consequences
- "What's your job/my job?"
- "What's my job if you don't follow the rules we agree on?"
- "What's the rule? Can you do it?"
- "What are you doing?"
- "That behavior won't work on me. Figure out something else."

Discuss the examples and procedures given in the handout "Classroom Rules" on page 44. Distribute the handout "Maintaining Limits" on page 45. Once the rules are established, teachers can maximize positive interactions with their students.

ACTIVITIES

▶ **My Job Is...** ☆

Discuss the following question: "What's my job if you don't follow the rules we agree on?" When we work with kids, we are involved with them in two ways: personal involvement, and role involvement. Role involvement describes the power relationships between two people due to their roles, regardless of the nature of the personal relationship. The phrases given below are useful when your personal involvement with a student interferes with the job to be done. Always use role involvement when in a discipline situation or when someone is attempting to verbally abuse you.

- *The rules is...*
- *The policy is...*
- *What we decided is...*

- *I'm in a position to...*
- *From my experience...*
- *That's not the issue. The issue is...*

1. *What's Your Job*
   With a partner or a small group, discuss the handout "What's Your Job?" on page 41. After the small group discussions, process with the large group.

2. *My Job Is...*
   With a partner or a small group, complete the handout "My Job Is..." on page 43. After the small group discussions, process with the large group. Use as a handout or transparency the sample "My Job Is..." on page 42.

3. *"My Job Is..." at All Levels*
   "My Job Is..." can be done at all levels throughout an organization. For example, among school board members and the superintendent, superintendent and princi-

pals, principals and teachers, fellow teachers, and teachers and students. The activity is even effective when done at home between parents and their children.

With a partner or in a small group, pick two roles from the ones listed above (e.g. student, teacher, parent, principle, etc.) and fill in the handout "My Job Is…" on page 43. Ask participants how they would do this exercise with their students of people they supervise.

▶ Classroom Rules

With a partner or in a small group, identify classroom rules that are consistent with Dr. William Glasser's guidelines in the handout "Rules for Rules" on page 46. After the small group discussions, process with the large group.

▶ Role Play: What's the Rule?

Pass out the handout "What's the Rule?" on page 47. Ask for a volunteer and demonstrate a role play in front of the group. Then have participants choose partners and perform their own role plays.

What's Your Job?

Discuss these questions with a colleague or your principal:

- Whose job is it to learn?

- Is it our job to motivate the students? Or is it our job to provide a safe, non-judg-mental environment in which they can motivate themselves?

- Is it our job to make students learn? Or is it our job to create the conditions for learning? Is it the students' job to learn?

- Is it our job to make students be nice to each other? Or is it our job to model awareness of other's needs for kindness and acceptance?

- Is it our job to make the students follow the rules? Or is it our job to tell them what we are obligated to do if they don't keep their commitment to the social con-tract?

Role: Teacher	**Role: Student**
My job is to... • Teach • Answer questions • Explain different ways • Teach at a pace at which you can learn • Manage the class • Enforce rules • Care about the students	**Your job is to...** • Learn • Ask if you don't understand • Keep on trying • Be there on time • Tell me if I go too fast • Follow the rules • Communicate your needs • Listen to others
My job is *not* to... • Make you learn • Take abuse • Baby-sit; taxi; lend money • Do your job	**Your job is *not* to...** • Do my job • Decide for another child • Discipline others

My Job Is...

Role:	**Role:**
My job is to...	**Your job is to...**
My job is *not* to...	**Your job is *not* to...**

Respect

*We believe it is important to respect all
people and their property.*

Work

*We believe it is important to work on tasks or
activities that have been assigned.*

Belong

*We believe it is important to belong to the
group and care about each other.*

- In order for students to take ownership of these three rules it is important to help define what each one means. At the beginning of the school year, as a class, brainstorm what each rule will look and sound like in the classroom and in different areas of the school (playground, cafeteria, hallways, etc.).

- To help students visualize this, take a sheet of chart paper and draw a line down the middle. At the top of the paper, write the rule. On one side, draw a pair of eyes, and on the other side, draw a pair of ears. As a class, describe what the rule looks like and what it sounds like. It is important to write down every comment so that all children feel they are a part of the process and will claim ownership.

- At the completion of this activity, each student should sign the chart paper and then it should be posted in the room.

*These rules were developed by Corwin Kronenberg, Lee Ann Wise, and Wise's
third grade class at Sheridan Hills Elementary School in Richfield, Minnesota.*

Once the rules are established, try to maximize positive interactions between yourself, as the teacher, and your students. Help students understand which behaviors are effective and which are ineffective when working with you.

This is how you get what you want from me:

- State your requests as questions.

- Ask me.

- Raise your hand.

- Speak clearly.

- Be pleasant.

- Use logic.

- Tell me what you need.

This doesn't work on me:

- Crying

- Whining

- Arguing

- Saying, "Everyone is doing it."

A rule needs to be stated in the positive

~

There should be few rules.
Children can't remember too many.

~

A rule must be enforceable; otherwise, drop it.

~

Be willing to change a rule if it doesn't work.

~

Children need to help make the rules and know them well.

~

When a rule is broken something must happen.

Guidelines provided by Dr. William Glasser

This exercise illustrates a technique used to focus on class expectations. This exercise shows the following:

- A way to save time
- The importance of minimizing conflict at the moment when a student misbehaves
- How to emphasize the solution rather than the problem
- How to use the "pause and thank you" technique
- How to avoid debate and excuses

1. Ask, "What's the rule?"

If the child doesn't know or won't say, repeat the rule yourself in the positive.

2. Ask, "Can't you do that?"

Don't require a verbal answer, a nod is adequate.

3. Pause, then say, "Thank you, I appreciate it."

By using this method you will avoid unnecessary confrontations. Stating a rule in the negative is ineffective because it emphasizes a failure identity. Stating a rule in positive builds on a success identity. Thus a student who has broken a rule is more likely to co-operate and less likely to act out or withdraw. Avoid moralizing, lecturing, or focusing on misbehavior. The child knows what he did. He made a social contract with the class. The question is, can he change his behavior?

MANAGING DIFFICULT SITUATIONS

8. REALITY THERAPY QUESTIONS

GOALS

▶ To use Reality Therapy questions as a vehicle for less coercive management of difficult children

▶ To differentiate between external and internal locus of control

REFERENCES

▶ *Restitution,* pages 82-87

▶ *Helping Disruptive and Unresponsive Students Video* with Diane Chelsom Gossen

HANDOUTS

▶ Reality Therapy Questions (page 51)

▶ What Are You Shooting For? (page 52)

FACILITATOR'S NOTES

▶ Reality Therapy, developed by Dr. William Glasser in 1965, is a positive, action-oriented approach to help people take more effective control of their lives. It teaches people to identify what they want, what they need, and what they are doing to get it. If their current behavior is not getting them what they want, they make a plan to change what they are doing.

▶ Using Reality Therapy, we teach children that we all have the same basic psychological needs—to be loved, to be successful, to have freedom of choice, and to have fun. We teach children that when they are upset it is because one of their needs is not being met.

▶ The children learn to figure out what they need—attention (love), achievement (power), independence (freedom), or laughter (fun). When children learn to identify the need they are not meeting, they can choose a better behavior which does not interfere with other people meeting their own needs.

▶ Reality Therapy questions are useful when managing difficult situations with students. I encourage you to teach your students these questions so they can ask them of each other.

- What do you want? What's the rule? *
- What are you doing? Saying?
- Is it working? Is it against the rule?
- Can you figure out a better way?

*Ask "What's the Rule?" in a discipline situation.

▶ If a student is unresponsive or defiant when asked a question, turn the question into a statement. Remember to use a calm, non-coercive tone of voice and carefully monitor your nonverbal message.

- "What do you want?"
  "This is what I need from you."

- "What are you doing?"
  "This is what I see/hear."

- "Is it working?"
  "It's not working for me."

- "Do you want to make a plan?"
  "This is what I want you to do."

These questions and statements are outlined on the handout "What Are You Shooting For?" on page 52.

ACTIVITY

▶ **Role Play: Reality Therapy Questions**
Distribute the handouts "Reality Therapy Questions" (page 51) and "What Are You Shooting For?" (page 52). Ask for a volunteer and demonstrate a role play in front of the group using the Reality Therapy questions. Then have participants choose partners and perform their own role plays.

The first role play scenario is between a teacher and a student who is willing to answer the posed questions. The second scenario is between a teacher and student who refuses to answer. The teacher must then pose the questions as statements.

Teachers are encouraged to teach their students these Reality Therapy questions so they can ask them of each other. If a student doesn't answer, the teacher turns the question into a statement.

What do you want? What's the rule?

This is what I need from you.

∽

What are you doing? Saying?

This is what I see/hear.

∽

Is it working? Is it against the rule?

It's not working for me.

∽

Can you figure out a better way?

This is what I want you to do.

What Are You Shooting For?

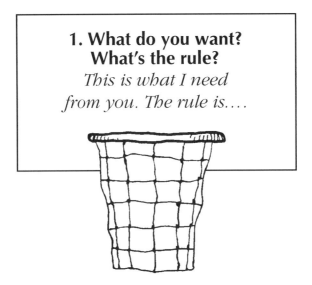

1. What do you want?
What's the rule?
This is what I need
from you. The rule is....

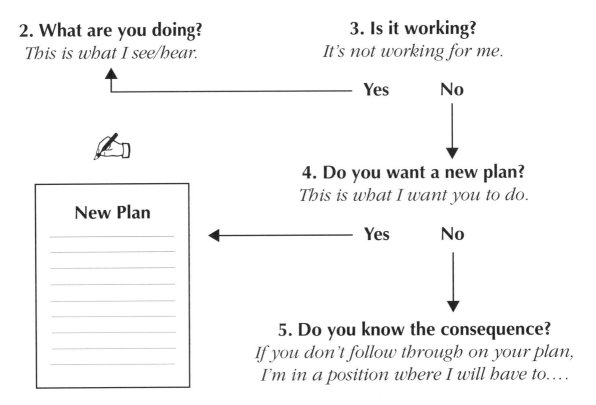

2. What are you doing?
This is what I see/hear.

3. Is it working?
It's not working for me.

Yes   No

New Plan

4. Do you want a new plan?
This is what I want you to do.

Yes   No

5. Do you know the consequence?
If you don't follow through on your plan,
I'm in a position where I will have to....

The text in larger print is what the teacher asks the student. If the student doesn't answer, the teacher turns the questions into statements. The statements are in italics.

This activity was inspired by Jim Montagnes.

9. WHEN TO DO WHAT

GOAL

▶ To learn various classroom management techniques for difficult situations

REFERENCE

▶ *Restitution*, pages 103-104

HANDOUT

▶ When to Do What (pages 55-56)

FACILITATOR'S NOTES

▶ **For the students:** If the primary focus of a restitution is on the victim, the locus of control is external. If the focus is on self-restitution, bringing oneself back to the person one wants to be, the locus of control is where we want it to be—internal. The art of Restitution is finding a creative way to practice self-restitution and as a by-product, making it right with the victim.

For the teacher: The art of Restitution is knowing when to do what, finding the time to do it, and knowing what to do if the student is uncooperative.

▶ There are a variety of effective classroom management techniques to use in difficult situations. These techniques vary significantly in the amount of time needed to process the activity with the child—some can be very time-consuming. However, there are many quick and simple management techniques (in the form of statements or questions that help to set the stage for Restitution. Some of these are:

- Yes, if...
- My job is..., Your job is...
- What's the rule? Can you do that?
- What are you doing?
- What do you want/need?
- How would you lie it to be?
- That behavior won't work on me. Figure out something else.

▶ These questions and statements shift the responsibility onto the student and set the stage for self-discipline.

▶ The chart "When To Do What" is designed to help answer three frequently asked questions:

- When do I do what?
- How can I find the time to help students make plans for restitution?
- What do I say if the student is unresponsive or defiant?

ACTIVITIES

▶ **Role Play: When To Do What**
Referring to the "When To Do What" handout on pages 55-56, role play various situations. Explore which classroom techniques are most effective. First, assume the student is responsive and cooperative. Then role play the same situation with a defiant student.

Classroom Techniques	With Unresponsive or Defiant Student
"Yes, if…" • When there *is* a choice • The "if" is possible • Give reason if the answer is "No"	
"What's your job? What's my job?" • When roles have previously been discussed • When student needs to refocus on job	
"What's the rule? Can you do that?" • In a discipline situation • When student knows the rule • When teacher needs to enforce the rule	**"What's the rule?" ["I don't know."]** • "The rule is…" ["I don't care."] • "Can you do it anyway?" [Silence plus nonverbal compliance.] • "Thank you. I appreciate it." [Don't hover; move on.]
"What are you doing?" • When student is unaware of what he's doing. • When you need more information • If student doesn't answer, give facts	**"What are you doing?"** • "What I see/hear you doing is…" [Silence.] • "Is it working for you?" ["Yes."] • "I understand…but it's not working for us. We need a better plan." [Wait for student to answer.]
"What do you want/need?" • When student is upset and you don't know why	**"What do you want/need?"** • "Why is it important to you?" • "How will it be better if you get what you want?" • "What does it mean to you?"
"How would you like it to be?" • When student complains • When student blames others	**"How would you like it to be?"** • "What do you want to be seeing?" • "What do you want to be hearing?" • "What do you think is a solution?"
"That behavior won't work!" • When student cries, whines, argues, says "Everyone is doing it."	**"This is how you get what you want from me."** • "Ask me." • "Tell me what you need."

Classroom Techniques	With Unresponsive or Defiant Student
Asking the Reality Therapy Questions • When student does not do what she needs to do to get what she wants. • When student needs to make a plan to help them get what they want. "What do you want? What's the rule?" "What are you doing? What are you saying?" "Is it working for you? Is it against the rule?" "Can you figure out a better way?"	**Asking the Reality Therapy Questions** • When a student is unresponsive or defiant, turn the question into a statement: "This what I need from you." "This is what I see." "It's not working for me." "This is what I want you to do."
Offering Student a Restitution Option • When student needs to fix something or make it right • When student want to make a self-restitution back to the kind of person he or she wants to be "What's the belief?" "What do you want to give back?" "Where?" "When?" • When the student does not want to make restitution, the teacher needs to use consequences: "What will happen if you keep doing this?"	**Offering Student a Restitution Option** • Remember, you can't force restitution. The words "have to" make restitution a consequence. • If the student does not want to make a restitution, say: "We want to work this out with you." "You're not the only one who's made a mistake." "You're basically a good kid. I think you can learn a better way to handle yourself." "If you don't want to learn to… [identify a better way], I'll be in a position where I have to… [identify consequence]. I don't want to do that. I want to work this out." [Leave the student to think about it and try later.]

Part II

Teaching Restitution

"Childhood is the most basic human right of children."

— David Elkind

10. IDENTITY CONCEPT

GOALS

▶ To understand the concept of identity

▶ To identify failure strategies we use when our needs aren't met

▶ To understand the importance of applying the concept of identity to yourself when not meeting your needs

▶ To understand how Restitution helps build a success identity by focusing on solutions, not misbehaviors

REFERENCES

▶ *Restitution,* pages 16-18

▶ *Schools Without Failure,* by Dr. William Glasser

HANDOUTS

▶ Identity Chart (page 61)

▶ My Success Strategies (page 62)

FACILITATOR'S NOTES

▶ Dr. William Glasser says that at any given time a person has either a failure identity or a success identity.*

▶ A success identity is maintained when a person feels good about the direction his life is going and is able to meet his needs for belonging, power, freedom, and fun without interfering with others meeting their needs.

▶ A failure identity is a result of the pain that comes from conflicting or unmet needs. A person with a failure identity feels bad about the direction his life is going. In order to deal with this pain we behave in one of two ways: fight (act out) or flight (withdraw). While these behaviors meet some of our needs, others are disrupted.

* *Since writing Control Theory, Dr. William Glasser is not using this concept. A deep understanding of Control Theory tells us all behavior is purposeful and no behaviors are "failure" behaviors. For the purpose of introducing teachers to punishment and discipline, this identity concept is quick and powerful.*

▶ People who are acting out use behaviors such as swearing, fighting, destroying things, stealing, or becoming sexually promiscuous.

▶ People who withdraw may have behaviors such as not answering, withdrawing to their rooms, not participating in activities, getting sick, daydreaming, sleeping a lot, using drugs or alcohol, or attempting suicide.

▶ Criticism and focusing on mistakes do not help people with failure identities. These practices only confirm their failures and keep them from learning new behaviors.

▶ When we ask the Reality Therapy questions and provide the opportunity to make a restitution, we help students create a success identity.

▶ Punishment does work in the short term on successful people. They can absorb it and, if their needs are being met, they are likely to forgive the punisher. Punishment does not work on a child who has a failure identity because this course of action merely confirms his feelings of inadequacy.

ACTIVITIES

▶ Brainstorm Failure Strategies ☆

Discuss acting out (fight) or withdrawing (flight) behaviors that you see students, as well as adults, use. Make a list for each type of behavior. Refer to the "Identity Chart" on page 61 for ideas.

▶ Personal Failure Strategies ☆

We all use ineffective behaviors at times—particularly when we are not meeting our needs. With a partner, identify which type of behavior you tend to use most—acting out or withdrawing. Discuss specific instances when you have chosen a failure identity. Remember that an awareness of these situations helps us choose more effective behaviors to meet our needs.

▶ Problem Students' Failure Strategies

Ask teachers to think of particular students that misbehave often. Discuss whether they tend to act out or withdraw. Which type of behavior causes the most discipline problems? Which type of student is at greatest risk?

▶ Brainstorm Success Strategies ☆

Ask participants what helps them maintain a success identity. Remind participants that these answers may seem somewhat "Pollyanna" or simplistic. Discuss and list the strategies that people use to be successful.

Use the handout "My Success Strategies" on page 62 to identify personal success behaviors. Also record how old you were when you learned each behavior and from whom you learned it (if applicable).

Some examples of success strategies include: initiating tasks, working hard, asking for help, being patient, taking one day at a time, going on when the going gets tough, being positive, saying "I need…."

When participants identify a behavior, ask them about their thoughts and actions. "What are you thinking when you use this strategy? What are you doing?" For example, one of my personal success strategies is to keep going when the going gets tough. When I use this strategy I *think* of my grandmother saying "Diane will bring home the bacon." What I *do* is try one more time or work for ten minutes more. This information is usually just below our level of awareness, so participants will need a moment to retrieve it.

Once several behaviors are identified, ask the question "If you use all these behaviors, are you likely to have problems meeting your needs? Will you be less likely to use behaviors which lead to a failure identity?"

Discuss how we can help students develop a success identity rather than reinforce a failure identity.

FAILURE	SUCCESS
People with failure identities attempt to meet their needs through ineffective behaviors. Examples include:	People with success identities meet the following needs through effective behaviors:

FAILURE

People with failure identities attempt to meet their needs through ineffective behaviors. Examples include:

Acting Out Behaviors (FIGHT)

- Fighting
- Swearing
- Complaining
- Destroying
- Stealing
- Sexual Promiscuity

Withdrawing Behaviors (FLIGHT)

- Not paying attention
- Threatening suicide
- Skipping school
- Being depressed
- Daydreaming
- Getting Sick
- Abusing drugs and alcohol
- Oversleeping

SUCCESS

People with success identities meet the following needs through effective behaviors:

NEEDS

Love/Belonging

- At least one person who cares about me in an unconditional accepting way
- Groups that accept me as a member
- Self-love, nurturing

Power/Competence

- The ability to create and maintain and impact on the world
- Things I do to feel capable
- Influencing others

Freedom

- Freedom from being manipulated
- Freedom to express myself
- Freedom to make my own decisions
- Availability of options

Fun

- Humor, laughing, jokes
- Activities that give me pleasure
- What I do when I don't have to

Physical

- Food, shelter, safety

My Success Strategies

Strategy	When I Learned It	Person(s) I Learned Behavior From
Example: Work hard	Age 6, chopping wood	My father

11. DIFFERENCES BETWEEN DISCIPLINE & PUNISHMENT

GOALS

▶ To identify the differences between discipline and punishment

▶ To encourage participants to practice self-discipline rather than punishment

REFERENCE

▶ *Restitution*, pages 16, 25-28

HANDOUT

▶ Differences Between Discipline & Punishment (page 65)

FACILITATOR'S NOTES

▶ Restitution, as a form of discipline, is the opposite of punishment.

▶ Discipline…

- Is reasonable and expected.
- Is a win-win process.
- Helps students learn better behaviors
- Helps to build better relationships.

▶ Punishment…

- Often injures both the offender and the victim.
- Tends to leave the offender feeling guilty or angry.
- Does not empower the offender to address the wrong and make a restitution
- Focuses on the problem rather than the solution.
- Does not help students overcome a failure identity.
- Belittles or hurts the person who has made the mistakes.

ACTIVITIES

▶ **Differences Between Discipline and Punishment**
Discuss the differences between discipline and Punishment. Be sure to relate punishment to the failure identity and discipline to the success identity. Refer to the handout "Differences Between Discipline & Punishment" on page 65. This may also be used as a transparency.

▶ A Time You Were Punished or Disciplined ☆

With a partner or in a small group, discuss a time when you were punished as a child. Then talk about a time when you were disciplined. This may be harder to remember because discipline—particularly self-discipline—is something that often happens subconsciously, without our awareness. (5 minutes for 2 people, 10 minutes for groups of 4 people)

Discussion points:

- Punishment can take the form of withdrawal of love.

- A participant may say, "My parents were tough with us, and I'm a better person for it." Punishment does work on successful people because they can absorb it and forgive the punisher. Punishment does not work on a child who has a failure identity because this course of action merely confirms his perceived inadequacy.

- To the teacher who defends punishment ask, "When you punish students do they act out or withdraw? Is that what you want? Are you interested in looking at another way to discipline students and help them achieve greater academic success?"

- Good discipline generally results in a better relationship between the adult and the child. However, no child will say at the moment of discipline, "Thank you very much, I know this will make me a better person." After a period of time the relationship will be stronger because the child will have a better understanding of the limits in the relationship and how he can fix his part of the problem.

▶ Enforcers

Pass out the handout "Differences Between Discipline & Punishment" on page 65. Discuss the "enforcers." Enforcers are strategies the teacher can use to enforce the rules. A parallel can be made with the laws of society. We have limited choices in enforcing our laws. We can increase the penalty, increase supervision, and redesign the system so that the problem disappears, or educate people.

Brainstorm about how a rule or law could be upheld by using each of the "enforcers" listed on the handout. For example, discuss the laws about driving while under the influence of alcohol. How could we redesign the system to better enforce these laws? Which countries have increased the penalty for drinking and driving? How do we increase supervision on the highway on New Year's Eve? How can we educate our youth about the reasons for these laws? Which strategy of law enforcement works best?

Now discuss a school example. Perhaps two classes are interacting in a rowdy manner when passing in the hall to the gym. We could increase the penalty for this to the point where the students lose their gym privileges or have detention. We could have extra adult supervision or redesign the schedules so that the classes would not pass each other in the hall. We could also educate the students about why we need speedy and safe movement in the halls and ask for their cooperation.

Differences Between Discipline & Punishment

DISCIPLINE	PUNISHMENT
Essential to building self-discipline and a success identity	Reinforces a failure identity; only works in the short term
Expected (consequences have been established)	Unexpected (punisher may be inconsistent)
Reasonable and fair	Too severe (in the eyes of society)
The child learns a better way or makes a restitution.	The child is subjected to anger, guilt, humiliation, or isolation.
Strengthens the relationship in the long run	Weakens the relationship in the long run—child withdraws or acts out

Enforcers

Discuss the different strategies given below.

MANAGER	MONITOR
Redesign the situation (time, space)	Increase the penalty (we tend to reach the maximum penalty quickly)
Educate (Discuss and clarify values)	Increase the supervision (staff does not like this)

12. DIFFERENCES BETWEEN CONSEQUENCES & RESTITUTION

GOAL

▶ To understand the differences between consequences and Restitution

REFERENCE

▶ *Restitution,* pages 59-62

HANDOUTS

▶ Differences Between Consequences and Restitution (page 68)

▶ Moving from Consequences to Restitution (page 69)

▶ Punishment, Consequences, and Restitution (pages 70-72)

FACILITATOR'S NOTES

▶ Traditional discipline procedures have been to impose consequences when people did not conform to the rules. Three kinds of consequences are listed below:

- Natural consequences occur in nature and are imposed by circumstances. An example would be walking in the rain and getting wet.

- Logical consequences are applied by the Monitor and are relevant.

- Chosen consequences occur when a person purposely does not fulfill his commitment. This occurs, for example, in a positive peer culture where the group determines sanctions for misbehavior and then enforces these consequences when necessary.

▶ Understanding consequences helps students make the connection between what they do and what happens as a result of their choices. Generally this connection is accomplished by age five. However, recent informal polls with teachers have indicated that many children come to kindergarten without an understanding of consequences. One of the reasons for this may be inconsistent management at home. Other reasons may be delayed development or attention-deficit problems. These children are not ready for restitution until they make this important connection.

▶ Consequences have a definite place in our lives. As a society, we impose consequences on those who do not follow our agreed upon laws. For example, illegally parking in a handicap zone can cost up to $600.00. It is important for a child to learn about and to experience consequences for misbehavior. Through this he will learn to conform to avoid pain. However, he will not learn to be a self-disciplined person unless he learns to fix his mistakes. The goal of Restitution is to strengthen the child by helping him learn to do this.

▶ Not all children will be ready to understand the Restitution process. Therefore, the school is strongly advised to keep rules in place. Both consequences and Restitution are forms of discipline, but only Restitution is self-discipline. While a chosen consequence may appear to be self-discipline, it is imposed within a stimulus-response context and does not lead to long-term positive growth. Therefore, because it does not strengthen the person, a chosen consequence is not Restitution.

ACTIVITIES

▶ **Differences Between Consequences and Restitution**
Discuss and list the differences between consequences and Restitution. Refer to the handout "Differences Between Consequences and Restitution" on page 68 for ideas. This handout may also be used as a transparency.

▶ **Moving from Consequences to Restitution**
Distribute the handout "Moving from Consequences to Restitution" on page 69. With a partner or a small group, follow the directions on the handout. Discuss as a large group.

▶ **Punishment, Consequences, and Restitution**
Preparation:

- For each group of two to four people, make one copy each of pages 70 and 71, and two copies of page 72.

- For each group, cut the copies of pages 70 and 71 into pieces and put the pieces into an envelope.

Directions:

- Each group of two to four people receives an envelope which contains the pieces of cut up paper. They also receive two copies of the "incomplete" version of "Punishment, Consequences, and Restitution" on page 72.

- Sort the pieces into three columns: Punishment, Consequences, and Restitution, and fill in the handout.

- Challenge groups to match the pieces going across the rows.

- The trainer may want to give participants a copy of the completed handout, "Punishment, Consequences, and Restitution" (pages 70-71) at the end of the sorting exercise. The emphasis is not to discover right or wrong answers, but rather to generate discussion within the group.

CONSEQUENCES	RESTITUTION
External evaluation	Self-evaluation
Rule *(What's the rule?)*	Belief *(What's the belief?)*
Discomforts the person	Strengthens the person
Imposed by authority	Invited and chosen by the subject
Expedient (takes less than 2 minutes)	Time-consuming (needs time for incubation and reflection)
Discussed and decided in advance	Created by or with the subject (and sometimes with the victim)
Reactive	Proactive

Choose an example of a discipline problem that can be dealt with by either imposing a consequence or planning a restitution. Illustrate the differences. An example is provided below.

Consequence

A daughter comes in at 12:00 a.m. Her curfew is 11:00 p.m. The consequence for getting home late is being grounded for the next weekend. The parents merely have to ask, "What time did we agree on?" and the daughter answers 11:00 (if she complies). The parents then say, "What happens now?" and the girl tells them that she's grounded for the next weekend. If the girl doesn't answer, the parents calmly provide the consequence. There is no need for further discussion, as it may lead to excuses and denial.

Restitution

Following the Restitution Model, the parents ask the daughter, "What does our family believe about letting each other know where we are?" The girl answers, "We keep each other informed." The parents then check to see if the belief is in place. "Do you still think this is important?" If the girl answers yes, the parents ask her to think about what should be done so that they do not have to worry and wait up for her in the future. If the girl answers no, they need to further discuss family beliefs. When the daughter focuses on what she can do to fix the problem, she is moving towards restitution.

YOUR OWN EXAMPLE:

Consequence _____

_____

Restitution _____

_____

FAILURE IDENTITY	SUCCESS IDENTITY	
PUNISHMENT	**DISCIPLINE**	
	Consequences	**Restitution**
Something hurtful must happen	Something must happen	Restitution is chosen
Uncomfortable for the child in the long run	Uncomfortable for the child in the short run	Comfortable for the child in the long run
The "victim" has justice	The "victim" may be ignored	The "victim" is compensated
Student is hurt	Student is inconvenienced	Student is strengthened
Passive-aggresive behavior escalates	The reinforcement only works short-term	Problems diminish
The system breaks down if students aren't afraid	Requires constant revision and supervision by the teacher	Student learns to take responsibility for own behavior
Works in an institution; doesn't carry over in the real world	Helps to establish and follow rules in society	Focus on long-term problem solving
The rule is…; You must….	*What's the rule? Can you do that? Thank you.*	*What do you believe? What can you do to fix it?*
Child resents the disciplinarian	Child respects the disciplinarian	Child respects himself and others
Negative	Neutral	Positive

FAILURE IDENTITY	SUCCESS IDENTITY	
	DISCIPLINE	
PUNISHMENT	**Consequences**	**Restitution**
Don't do it again, or else....	*Do what I tell you to do.*	*Is this what you want to be doing?*
Coercion mode	Stimulus-response	Control theory
Encourages self-criticism	Encourages conformity	Encourages self-discipline
Bad self-concept	Good self-concept	Strong self-concept
Child learns to hide mistakes	Child learns to follow rules	Child learns to solve problems
We try to control the child by negative reinforcement ("An eye for and eye...")	We try to control the child by positive reinforcement	Child understands that he controls himself
Anger, guilt, humiliation, withdrawal of approval	Time-out, loss of privilege, detention	Child does not lose anything but invests energy to make reparation
Unexpected or too severe consequences	Expected, reasonable, consequences	Invited restitution
Developed by the teacher	Developed by the teacher and the child	Developed by the child
Hurts—Teacher applies the consequences along with mor-alizing, criticizing, sarcasm	Helps—Teacher asks or states the rule, gives a warning and then applies the consequence	Strengthens—Teacher recalls social contract; sets frame of reference for restitution by child

FAILURE IDENTITY	SUCCESS IDENTITY	
PUNISHMENT	**DISCIPLINE**	
	Consequences	Restitution

13. RESTITUTION CONCEPTS

GOAL

▶ To understand the Restitution concepts

REFERENCE

▶ *Restitution,* pages 43-49

HANDOUTS

▶ Self-Restitution (page 75)
▶ Restitution Is a Daily Event (page 76)

FACILITATOR'S NOTES

▶ There is no correct order in which to learn Restitution. Some of the Restitution concepts may already be in a teacher's repertoire. For example, many teachers have heard themselves say, "It's OK to make a mistake." Intuitively, we have known that this eases a student's guilt even though we may not have recognized that this technique stabilizes the student's success identity and sets the stage for making a restitution. As you read this information:

  • Examine the model
  • Recognize the pieces you are already using
  • Experiment with new techniques
  • Apply the model holistically and flexibly

▶ Restitution is a different mental model. The Restitution model focuses on strengthening the offender, whereas retribution, which is practiced by today's justice system, focuses on hurting the offender and sometimes making reparation to the victim. Restitution, as taught in this facilitator's guide, focuses on self-reparation by the offender. As a result of self-reparation, restitution is made to the victim.

▶ Restitution refutes stimulus-response thinking. The Restitution Model contradicts most practices recommended in schools today. School procedures tend to be grounded in stimulus-response theory—with a strong emphasis on initially rewarding the child's appropriate behavior, then withholding the reward when the child "misbehaves." Discomforting the child is a valid form of discipline if it is reasonable and expected, but it will not help the child learn self-discipline. Restitution, on the other hand, is based on the Control Theory belief that we are internally motivated. Therefore, the only effective form of discipline in the long term is self-discipline.

▶ What is Restitution? Restitution is the action of repairing a damage done. It is about making things right. It is the opportunity for an individual who has made a mistake to make full reparation to the best of her ability. It enables the individual to reclaim self-esteem through personal effort. This process helps the person become stronger than she was before she erred. This is the real power of the process.

ACTIVITIES

▶ **Self-Restitution** ☆
The purpose of this activity is to encourage participants to begin thinking about how their idea of restitution differs from or coincides with the concepts in the book *Restitution*. With a partner or in a small group, discuss the handout "Restitution" on page 75.

▶ **Restitution Is a Daily Event** ☆
With a partner or in a small group, read and discuss the situations in the handout "Restitution Is a Daily Event" on page 76. After the small group discussions, process with the large group.

Self-Restitution

When thinking about the concept of restitution, most people generally think of restitution to the victim. While this is important, the major focus needs to be on self-restitution, where offenders restore themselves back to the persons they want to be. Restitution is mostly about gaining self-balance.

Each of us has pictures in our heads of the way we want things to be. The higher level pictures reflect the values we hold. These pictures are like mental magnets—they pull our behavior to match what we have decided is important. I have pictures about myself as a caring, competent, and responsible person who is always growing and self-actualizing. When I perceive myself to be out of balance I seek to restore myself back to the person I picture myself to be.

This process of restoring oneself is an ongoing self-reparation. Successful people make restitution to themselves all the time. Often it is almost automatic, as clever and efficient as our system is. Restitution may be as simple as stepping back in line and letting someone go ahead of us if we find we have cut them off. The Restitution process is a creative art and is especially challenging when the reparation is not immediately evident.

DISCUSSION QUESTIONS

- How do you define *restitution*?

- How does the above explanation of *restitution* differ from yours?

- How does the above explanation of *restitution* coincide with yours?

We all have pictures of ourselves as people who can contribute and carry a share of the load in different situations. When we perceive ourselves to be less than adequate in this area, we make an adjustment. For example, I was presenting a workshop at a school and as I got out of the front passenger seat I noticed my driver struggling to lift my workshop materials from the back seat. In a flash I opened the back door on my side and said, "Can I carry your books?" She answered, "No, those are not for this workshop." Although I was unable to complete my proposed restitution, I personally felt restored having made the offer. The restitution I offered was generated in less than a second as my right brain grasped the situation, and it restored my self-esteem.

SHARED RESPONSIBILITY

Sometimes I insist on paying my share of a bill. If a friend has treated me too often I say, "I need to do this for myself." Think of an example where you recently made a restitution with regard to shared responsibility. Share this with a partner.

TIME AND COMMITMENT

In our family we believe that we should let each other know where we are. When I am delayed and I fail to inform my family, I feel out of balance. I am not being the person I want to be. Once in a while I rationalize it. More often I make a self-restitution. This is also the behavior I want from my family. Think of an example when you made a restitution with regard to time and commitment.

PROPERTY DAMAGE

Have you ever made a reparation for property damage? I recently replaced a punch bowl I broke. I felt much better when I made this restitution. How about you? Any examples?

LABOR

Consider a restitution for labor. I recently did the dishes after someone made a meal for me. I insisted on it because I had been a guest many times and fortunately my host accepted. Think of an example where someone served you and you returned the favor. Why did you do this?

COMMUNICATION

Imagine a scenario in which you inadvertently said something that led to a colleague's embarrassment. Perhaps you shared information with others that your colleague did not want revealed. Are you aware of how rapidly your system attempts to create a restitution? In situations like these your brain works overtime to generate a plan for restitution. Why would you do that? Partly for your colleague, but more importantly to restore yourself. You picture yourself as a trustworthy, supportive friend. By making it right with your colleague, you gain self-balance. Think of an example from your life where you made a verbal restitution in a public forum. Think small—the offense is probably not glaring. Share your example with a partner.

14. CHARACTERISTICS OF A RESTITUTION

GOAL

▶ To understand the characteristics of Restitution

REFERENCES

▶ *Restitution*, pages 49-63

▶ *Restitution Staff Development Video Series:* Tape IV, "Characteristics of Restitution"

HANDOUTS

▶ "Snowballs" Example (page 80)

▶ "Learning To Sew" Example (page 81)

▶ "A Better Way to Treat You" Example (page 82)

▶ "Plant the Seed" Example (page 83)

▶ Reflecting on Characteristics from Stories (page 84)

FACILITATOR'S NOTES

▶ **Characteristics of Restitution: What to Observe**

These characteristics are indicators that the process underway is self-discipline, not consequences or punishment.

1. **Strengthens the Person Who Has Offended**

   The offender is strengthened when…

   • He is eager to make a restitution.
   • His tone is confident.
   • He does not avoid making eye contact.
   • He smiles at the end of the restitution.
   • He wants to share what he or she has done.
   • He feels positive about himself and the school.
   • He frequently suggests something else to contribute.
   • He brings up another unresolved problem to solve.

   If the student is apathetic, guilt-ridden, mumbling, downcast, or unresponsive, Restitution is not in process.

2. Tied to a Higher Value or the Mission Statement

What does it mean for a restitution to be tied to a higher value? To understand how to recognize this characteristic of Restitution refer back to the Social Contract (pages 33-37). If you have not made a social contract with your class, Restitution will be effective with only those students who have family beliefs similar to the school's. All families have implicit higher level values in place. However, they may not be the desired values of the school. If we want students to operate by our set of values, the teacher will have to explore them with the group. It is not the job of the teacher to criticize the home. It is the job of the teacher to help children gain new pictures of how they might interact. From our experience the highest level of values we develop with children at school are seldom in conflict with parents because they are consistent with society's values and reflect the universal golden rule. Examples of such values are listed on page 35.

3. Satisfactory Amends to the Victim

What is a satisfactory amend? Sometimes the victim will be consulted to create the restitution. Ideally the victim will be satisfied with the restitution offered. However, if the restitution has been created and offered in good faith and the victim clearly rejects it, the teacher should mediate and help the offender understand that his self-restitution is not dependent on the victim's acceptance.

4. Effort Required from the Offender

The child needs to invest thought, time, and energy toward the solution to the problem. Effort does not mean discomfort to the child by an external force. Making the football team run two extra laps when they have played poorly is not the type of effort required. Most effort of this type is expended with a negative "I'll show you" mind set. The effort needed for a restitution must be proactive and come voluntarily from the offender.

5. Relevant to the Offense Whenever Possible

In delivering a relevant restitution the following issues need to be considered:

- The effort required should be commensurate with the offense. Discipline must be reasonable, not excessive.

- The aim of the restitution needs to be restoring the offender back to the person he wants to be, as well as repairing the damage done to the victim.

Frequently schools have their favorite chores which they prescribe for offenders. Examples are picking up garbage in the yard, cleaning cafeteria tables, or cleaning chalk erasers. These are *not* restitutions because they are mandated and seldom relevant to the offense.

6. Little Incentive for Repetition of the Offense

The teacher needs to be aware that if a victim enjoys the restitution, he may purposely aggravate the offender to misbehave again. For example, a child teases another child. As a restitution, the offender offers a cookie to his victim. The next day, the victim, who seldom gets sweets in his lunch, tries to provoke the offender to tease him again so that he will be offered another cookie. In this situation, the teacher needs to ask each child about the classroom beliefs about respect. They then need to evaluate whether the restitution is helpful or exploitative.

ACTIVITIES

▶ **Example for You to Analyze: "Snowballs"**
See the handout on page 80. Have participants read the example and examine the characteristics of restitution for this example. [Note: the "Snowballs" example in the handout on page 80 is an abbreviated version of the "Snowballs" example in *Restitution*; for the full text, see pages 52-55 of *Restitution*.]

▶ **Example for You to Analyze: "Learning To Sew"**
See the handout on page 81. Have participants read the example and examine the characteristics of restitution for this example.

▶ **Example for You to Analyze: "A Better Way to Treat You"**
See the handout on page 82. Have participants read the example and examine the characteristics of restitution for this example.

▶ **Example For You To Analyze: "Plant the Seed"**
See the handout on page 83. Have participants read the example and examine the characteristics of restitution for this example.

▶ **Reflecting on Characteristics from Stories**
Discuss the learning points given on page 84 with workshop participants.

"Snowballs" Example

In Saskatchewan, where we have a lot of snow in the winter, I live in a flat-roofed house. One day I hired my twelve-year-old son and his friend to shovel the roof for $10. Suddenly there was a knock at my door and a very angry man informed me that two kids on my roof were throwing ice balls. I called the boys down from the roof and said to them, "This is not what I want to be hearing—that two boys are throwing icy snowballs at cars. What you did could have hurt people. What do we believe about safety in our family?" I struggled to move away from my anger toward restitution. I haltingly framed my request, "Figure out what you can do to make this right. What you did could have hurt people, so you need to figure out something to do to help people—and it has to have something to do with ice and snow." They responded, "Just don't give us the $10." I said, "No, that's not good enough. The issue here is not the money, the issue is throwing icy snowballs that could have caused an accident or a broken windshield. You need to figure out how to make amends." Over the next hour and a half, there was a series of phone calls back and forth between Sam and Jake. Finally, Sam arrived at the door with a bag of ice salt and I relaxed knowing that a solution was in progress. The boys would go over to Jake's elderly baby-sitter's house, clean her walk, and put ice salt on it. Then they would go to Sam's grandpa's home to clean the ice off his windows so he could get out if there were a fire. The boys then said, "You need to drive us." I replied, "This is not my restitution! You need to find your own way over there. Here's the number of the transit system for the schedule. I'll give you the bus fare." After another half-hour of planning they were on their way. Three hours later they returned triumphant with stories: Sam cut his hand on the sharp ice (Dreikurs would call this "natural consequences," I called it "poetic justice"); the elders were grateful; and the boys were proud of negotiating the bus transfers. They had learned, they were strengthened, and the odds were they would think twice about throwing icy snowballs again.

In this example, which of the characteristics of restitution were present?

_____ 1. Strengthens the person who has offended

_____ 2. Tied to a higher value or to the person one wants to be.

_____ 3. Satisfactory amends to the victim

_____ 4. Effort required from offender

_____ 5. Relevant to the offense (whenever possible)

_____ 6. Little incentive for repetition of the offense

_____ 7. No resentment by the planner/helper

_____ 8. No criticism, guilt, or anger

Two fourth-grade boys scuffled on the playground. Evert grabbed Thomas and ripped three buttons off his shirt. The playground supervisor sent them in to speak to the principal. The principal reminded Evert about the school's belief in respect for each other. She asked Evert if he would be willing to make up to Thomas for what he had done. He nodded. She then asked Thomas what he wanted. Thomas said, "I need my buttons fixed. My mom's going to kill me!" The principal asked Evert if he'd be willing to sew Thomas' buttons back on. Outraged, Evert retorted, "I don't know how to sew!" She asked him if he would be willing to learn to sew. He answered, "Who will teach me?" She said, "The teaching assistant." Evert agreed and spent the noon hour learning to sew and repairing Thomas' shirt. Last seen, Thomas was arm-in-arm with Evert on the playground.

In this example, which of the characteristics of restitution were present?

_____   1. Strengthens the person who has offended

_____   2. Tied to a higher value or to the person one wants to be.

_____   3. Satisfactory amends to the victim

_____   4. Effort required from offender

_____   5. Relevant to the offense (whenever possible)

_____   6. Little incentive for repetition of the offense

_____   7. No resentment by the planner/helper

_____   8. No criticism, guilt, or anger

A class of middle-school students acted rudely to a substitute teacher. They talked continuously while she was attempting to teach the class, and when she tried to address them, they laughed. Three girls were targeted as the culprits. When their teacher returned to school, she confronted them with the note from the substitute teacher and asked them what they could do to make a restitution. The girls debated a bit, then offered to apologize. The teacher said they could do so if they wished, then asked them what they could do to make a restitution. They made the evaluation that their behavior was not in line with the school's beliefs. The girls proposed that they could initiate a discussion with the rest of their classmates about how they should behave next time. Then they would write a letter to the substitute teacher informing her of their decision. They would also tell her that they were writing a letter to the principal to request her as a substitute the next time their teacher was away in order to behave better.

In this example, which of the characteristics of restitution were present?

_____   1. Strengthens the person who has offended

_____   2. Tied to a higher value or to the person one wants to be.

_____   3. Satisfactory amends to the victim

_____   4. Effort required from offender

_____   5. Relevant to the offense (whenever possible)

_____   6. Little incentive for repetition of the offense

_____   7. No resentment by the planner/helper

_____   8. No criticism, guilt, or anger

"Plant the Seed" Example

A fifth-grade student, while playing with matches, accidentally torched a field containing twenty seedlings our class had planted, destroying them all. I asked him to come up with a plan for fixing the problem and he suggested that he could replant the seedlings. I went with him to get the trees and he planted them on his own time. He was a very bright student but had some behavior problems. After this he had a more positive attitude towards school.

In this example, which of the characteristics of restitution were present?

_____ 1. Strengthens the person who has offended

_____ 2. Tied to a higher value or to the person one wants to be.

_____ 3. Satisfactory amends to the victim

_____ 4. Effort required from offender

_____ 5. Relevant to the offense (whenever possible)

_____ 6. Little incentive for repetition of the offense

_____ 7. No resentment by the planner/helper

_____ 8. No criticism, guilt, or anger

| **HANDOUT** | **Reflecting on Characteristics from Stories** |

Discuss the following learning points with workshop participants. You can learn a lot about how to implement Restitution by looking at examples of restitution plans. The stories listed below include important learning points.

1. "The Air Pump" (*Restitution*, pages 58-59)

   Learning Point: Self-restitution will not take place if the child is guilt-ridden. For more information on how to help a child stop feeling guilty, see page 103 on stabilizing the identity.

2. "Learning To Sew" (*Restitution*, pages 56-57)

   Learning Point: Restitution teaches new behaviors. When freely chosen by the child, Restitution provides the energy and motivation to learn new skills.

3. "A Better Way To Treat You" (*Restitution*, pages 57-58)

   Learning Point: A common pitfall in applying Restitution is to accept apologies in lieu of reparation. An apology is not a restitution for several reasons. First, using the word *sorry* can imply "I'm wretched, I'm miserable." This interpretation puts the person in a failure identity. Many times students say bad things about their own behavior to head off adults saying these same things. This does not build good self-esteem. Second, an apology does not provide information about what the child will do next time to amend the situation. Third, some children are masters at making apologies—they have made the practice a highly developed art form. They gain temporary relief but do not get stronger.

4. The "Wayward Trio" (*Restitution*, pages 110-111) and "The Guest Reader" (*Restitution*, pages 111-112)

   Learning Point: There are three important learning points in each of these stories. First, the teacher clearly stated the expectation up front, asking the children what they thought was expected of them. Sometimes this is better if resistance is expected. In each case the children knew the expectation so there was a quick shift to restitution rather than defensive denial. Second, the focus was on future contributions to the group rather than on past irresponsibility. Third, the restitution resulted in the children learning new behaviors that they could continue to use.

15. FRAMING UP A RESTITUTION

GOALS

▶ To define the three locators of a restitution

▶ To identify the process to help students frame up a restitution

REFERENCE

▶ *Restitution,* pages 48-49

HANDOUTS

▶ Locators of Restitution (page 87)

▶ Framing Up Restitution (page 88)

FACILITATOR'S NOTES

▶ Planning and making a restitution is a creative art. It is the job of the teacher to help students frame up the restitution which considers both the victim's needs and the offender's needs. For example, "What could you do to give back to the class some of the time you have used up without having to miss the after-school activity?" or "What could you do to repair that broken equipment that won't cost your dad money?"

▶ Often children will initially answer that a restitution is impossible because they do not see an immediate solution. However, if we are patient, ask the question again, frame up the conditions, and give them some time, they are generally able to come up with very creative ideas.

▶ If they can't come up with a suggestion, then the teacher can offer a possibility. Usually when there is difficulty with a solution it is because we are looking too concretely and focusing on the offense rather than focusing on strengthening the child and providing an opportunity for him to contribute to the group. Allow the child time to think on his own to create a restitution. This process is an invitation, not a demand; it cannot be rushed.

▶ Explain the three locators:

Belief: Identify the belief that has been violated. Refer back to the beliefs established in the social contract. Ask the child, "What kind of a person do you want to be?"

Category: Establish the context or category of the violation. Identify the how, where, who, or what of the offense. Ask the child, "What do you want to give back to the person?" or "How do you want to fix it?"

Time Frame: Establish when the child will make the restitution.

▶ Distribute the handout "Locators of Restitution" on page 87. Discuss the three locators and the restitution questions.

Three locators of a restitution

- Belief is connected.
- Category is established.
- Time frame is set.

Restitution questions

- What's the belief?
- Who is the person you want to be?
- What do you want to give back to that person?
- Where?
- When?

When the restitution is complete, ask the person to self-evaluate. "What does it say about you that you decided to fix this?"

ACTIVITY

▶ **Framing Up Restitution**
Refer to the book *Restitution* to complete this activity. Distribute the handout "Framing Up Restitution" on page 88. Discuss the first example as a large group. Identify the belief, category, and time frame for the restitution described in the "Snowballs" example (*Restitution*, pages 52-55). With a partner or in a small group, participants should identify the belief, category, and time frame for the other two examples: "Learning To Sew" (*Restitution*, pages 56-57) and "The Wayward Trio" (*Restitution*, pages 110-111).

After the small group discussions, process as a large group. Below is the answer key to this activity:

Learning to Sew (*Restitution* pages 56-57): *Belief*—Respect for another's property; *Category*—The shirt (clothing); *Time Frame*—Noon.

The Wayward Trio (*Restitution* pages 110-111): *Belief*—Each person is important to the quality of the whole group; *Category*—Doing something (activity) for the group; *Time Frame*—Now, tonight.

Locators of a Restitution

Belief is connected.

Category is established.

Time frame is set.

Restitution Questions

What's the belief?

Who is the person you want to be?

What do you want to give back to that person?

Where?

When?

Another way to begin forming a restitution is to talk to the person who has the problem about the need that they violated for the other person or for the group. Sometimes it is difficult to repair a mistake. In this case, it is important to teach youth about their basic needs. We use William Glasser's needs of love, power, freedom, fun and survival. We ask the student, "What need of the person do you think you violated by what you did or said?" For example, if a person is enclosed from a group activity the need would be belonging, if a person is criticized, the need would be power. Many restitution options are opened up if we say to the student, "What can you do to include that person at recess this afternoon?" or, "What honest thing can you say to give back some power to the person you criticized?"

Framing Up Restitution

When a direct restitution cannot be made, it is necessary to "frame up" the direction in which to seek a creative restitution. To do this, we must isolate the important variables of a solution. The variables are placed as locators in the right brain—the creative hemisphere of the brain. We can then create a plan for restitution. For each of the following examples:

1. Identify the *belief* which has been violated (high level of perception).

2. Set the *category* or context in which the restitution will be made (limiting condition).

3. Establish a *time frame*. The younger the person, the shorter the time frame (preferably within 24 hours).

▶ **Example: Snowballs *(Restitution* pages 55-52)**

- Belief: "What you did could have hurt someone, therefore you need to help someone."

- Category: "It has to do with ice and snow."

- Time Frame: "And you need to do it before dark today."

▶ **Learning to Sew *(Restitution* pages 56-57)**

- Belief _____

- Category _____

- Time Frame _____

▶ **The Wayward Trio *(Restitution* pages 110-111)**

- Belief _____

- Category _____

- Time Frame _____

16. THE RESTITUTION TRIANGLE

GOALS

▶ To understand that the process of Restitution strengthens the child who has made a mistake

▶ To understand that all behavior is purposeful

REFERENCES

▶ *Restitution,* pages 45-49, 107-109, 118-120

▶ *Restitution Staff Development Video Series:* Tape II, "The Restitution Triangle"

HANDOUTS

▶ The Restitution Triangle (page 94)

▶ Could You Have Done Worse? (page 95)

▶ Identity Tune-Up (page 96)

FACILITATOR'S NOTES

▶ Use as a handout or a transparency "The Restitution Triangle" on page 94. The Restitution Triangle is the process by which a teacher or parent helps prepare a child for Restitution. The process includes three steps and each is grounded in an important principle of Control Theory (in italics).

  1. Stabilize the identity – *We are doing the best we can.*
  2. Validate the misbehavior – *All behavior is purposeful.*
  3. Seek the belief – *We are internally motivated.*

These three strategies represent the three sides of the Restitution Triangle. When helping to frame a restitution, you do not need to use each strategy every time. Many teachers already use versions of these strategies in their own personal management styles without knowledge of the Restitution Triangle.

▶ **Side 1: Stabilize the Identity**

Making mistakes is part of the learning process.
The base of the triangle deals with shifting the identity of the child from failure to success. The child who is acting out or withdrawing is experiencing a failure identity. He is trying to meet his needs but is in conflict. If we criticize him, we keep him in this

position. If we want to be proactive, we need to intentionally counteract this trend by reassuring the child.

- It's OK to make a mistake.
- Perfection is not a human condition.
- I've made that mistake too.
- We can solve this.
- I'm not interested in the mistake. I'm interested in it being fixed.
- You have a right to your feelings.
- Are you being a good friend to yourself?

When we make these statements, it is very difficult, if not impossible, for the child to remain withdrawn or rebellious. Playground supervisors report that this investment of 30 seconds turns many adversarial situations into cooperative ones.

It is also very difficult, if not impossible, to make restitution if the offender is focused on guilt. There are three reasons for this. First, guilt takes energy. Feeling guilty takes about the same amount of energy that could be used to solve a problem. Second, when we feel guilty we experience a failure identity. In this mode, one tends to choose blame or denial rather than reparation. Third, guilt keeps us anchored in the past where we have no control. We cannot impact on what has already happened. We can only impact on the present and future. Momentary feelings of guilt alert us when we are out of balance. The feelings tell us that a behavior is not matching a self-picture we hold dear. The moment we feel the flush of guilt we need to be proactive and move to the process of restitution.

▶ Side 2: Validate the Misbehavior

Every misbehavior is meeting a need.
Control Theory tells us that all behavior is purposeful. Every behavior—whether "good" or "bad"—is better than another behavior we might have chosen. A teacher who understands Control Theory will purposely shift herself from the stimulus-response mind set to a proactive mind set which recognizes the purposefulness of the child's behavior. We may not like it when a child whines, but if the behavior gets our attention it is need-satisfying for the child. Recognizing this will establish rapport with the child. The following comments may seem foreign to the teacher, but when delivered in a non-judgmental tone of voice they will help to validate the misbehavior.

- You could have done worse.
- You didn't do that for no reason.
- Give yourself credit for protecting something that was important to you.
- Keep that behavior but add another one, a new behavior.

Teachers usually tell a child to give up a bad behavior, but Control Theory tells us such a prescription is not possible. We will always remember the behaviors we learn, "good" or "bad," and will always be able to access them.

For example, consider a child who has been told by his parents that fighting is a good behavior. Traditional dialogue on the playground would go something like this: "Stop fighting. That is a bad behavior. Don't do it again. You should have done better." Control Theory tells us to be proactive in a different direction.

Teacher: "Were you fighting? Do you know how to fight?" *(Is the behavior in his repertoire?)*

Child: "Yes."

Teacher: "Do I need to teach you to fight?"

Child: "No, my dad taught me."

The teacher will then make a very powerful proactive statement.

Teacher: "It's good that you know that behavior; sometimes in life you might need it. *(Validates the misbehavior.)* Do you need me to help you remember how to fight?"

Child: "No."

Teacher: "Would you be willing to learn another way to get what you want without hitting?"

Now the child is in a position to learn a new behavior without giving up what he knows. We always ask a person to add behaviors rather than to delete them. Another conversation might go like this:

Teacher: "Is fighting helping?"

Child: "Yes."

Teacher: "How?"

Child: "He stopped teasing me."

Teacher: "So fighting worked somewhat (*validates the misbehavior*), but here you are in time-out. Is this where you want to be?"

Child: "No."

Teacher: "Do you need to figure out a way to stop teasing and keep your recess?"

It may appear that validating the misbehavior contradicts and invalidates the rules decided by staff. *We do not ask teachers to say misbehavior is good behavior.* We merely suggest they recognize the purposefulness of it, understanding that each person is doing the best they can at the moment. A misbehavior is usually very satisfying to the child's need for power or freedom but often interferes with his need for belonging. If we reject him, we become part of the problem. If we validate him as a person, he feels recognized and understood. Teachers who have tried this strategy report that students who were previously unreachable have opened up to these questions. This strategy is mutually beneficial to the teacher and the student as the teacher must stand in the shoes of the child and therefore gains an added dimension of perception.

▶ Side Three: Seek the Belief

Control Theory tells us that we are internally motivated. Once the misbehavior has been validated and the success identity stabilized, the student is ready to tie his beliefs to his misbehavior and move towards becoming the kind of person he wants to be. (My colleague, Barnes Boffey, calls this process "Reinventing Yourself.) The following questions tie the student's beliefs to those of the class or family. Refer back to the social contract.

- What do we, as a class (or family), believe?
- What are the common values we agreed on?
- What is our picture of an ideal classroom?
- What kind of a person do you want to be?

E. Perry Good, in her book *Helping Kids Help Themselves*, provides good ideas about how adults can help their own children or students. It is important to ask children questions about the overall direction they are taking their lives. For example, "Do you want to be a person who is successful, responsible, and trustworthy?" Most children will answer yes, but they don't know how to become these things. The teacher can then ask the student what it would look like (or be like) if she were that person. Once the child has a clear picture of the person she wants to be, the teacher can help the child maintain a focus on this picture.

For activities which focus on beliefs, see "Gaining Consensus—The Social Contract" on pages 33-37.

ACTIVITIES

▶ Activity for Restitution Triangle, Side 1: Be Your Own Best Friend

1. Divide the group into two teams, a positive team and a negative team.

2. Brainstorm and create lists of negative and positive statements about a hypothetical person.

3. For each negative statement made by the negative team the other side counters with a positive statement.

4. Make a list of the negative statements ("Put Downs") and a list of positive statements ("Uppers").

5. Individuals can then make up their own "Best Friend" lists of positive statements to encourage and affirm themselves.

▶ **Activity for Restitution Triangle, Side 2: Could You Have Done Worse?**

Pass out the handout "Could You Have Done Worse" on page 95. Invite participants to do the activity.

▶ **Activity for Restitution Triangle, Side 3: Identity Tune-Up** ☆

Pass out the handout "Identity Tune-Up" on pages 96. Invite participants to do the activity.

The Restitution Triangle

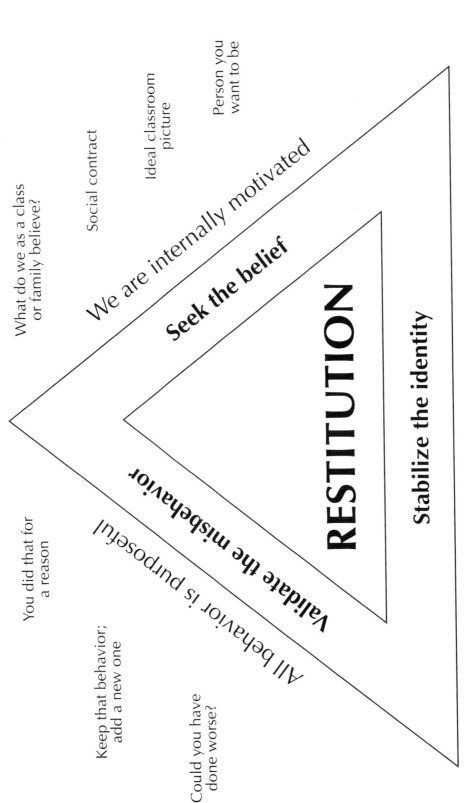

What do we as a class or family believe?

Social contract

Ideal classroom picture

Person you want to be

We are internally motivated

Seek the belief

You did that for a reason

Keep that behavior; add a new one

Could you have done worse?

All behavior is purposeful

Validate the misbehavior

RESTITUTION

Stabilize the identity

We are doing the best we can

Perfection is not a human condition

You're not the only who's made that mistake

It's OK to make a mistake

I'm not interested in fault

Be a good friend to yourself

© 1997 Diane Chelsom Gossen

Could You Have Done Worse?

Ask each participant to find a partner. Each participant should think of a situation where he feels that the behavior he chose was not a good one; where he has a bad feeling about the choice in retrospect. The partner must then ask the following questions:

1. What was the situation? What behavior did you choose?

2. Could you have done worse? Here the partner will probably have to probe, challenge, and question further. First, the partner can exaggerate a worse behavior, using humor. For example: "Instead of pushing the victim, you could have punched." Second, the helper can go in the opposite direction. For example: "So you lost your temper. Would it have been better not to have attempted to address the issue? What would that have meant about you as a person?" The helper pursues this track until the person understands that he made that choice in order to avoid a worse option. When this happens, there is a lifting of guilt and a rise in positive energy.

3. What did you want at that time? How was it important to you? What need(s) were you trying to fulfill? What kind of person were you trying to be?

4. Are you giving yourself credit for protecting something important to you? What was the value you were trying to protect? Do you realize that it was the best you could figure out at the time? When the person recognizes this, they are ready to make a new action plan.

5. The helper looks for a value judgment. "Do you want to figure out a better way for next time?" Continually validate the misbehavior. Say, "It worked somewhat, but is that the kind of person you want to be? How does this tie in with your beliefs?" Talk about beliefs and values established in the social contract. Don't say, "Stop that behavior." Say, "Keep that behavior but add another one, a new behavior."

On a continuum, this process moves the person from failure to success by expanding the continuum of negative options.

The mind set with which a restitution is made is more important than the restitution itself. One's mind set, with a focus on becoming the person you want to be, is the key to whether one builds character or resentment.

An Example

Last summer I phoned Neil at home. When I asked him what he was doing, he said, "I'm watering your flowers." I asked, "And how is it watering my flowers? You like the flowers too. Consider doing it because you enjoy their beauty and want to nourish them." That's about all the counseling I can get away with among my family, so I dropped the subject but could not resist asking when I got home if the mind shift had been made. It had. Did it make a difference? It did, even though the task was exactly the same. Neil had three choices of mind set:

- Anger at me (acting out)
- Fear of being reprimanded (withdrawal)
- Doing the job for himself (a success identity)

School Application

When a student makes a plan for restitution, ask her to identify her thoughts and actions. For example, if a student decides that as a restitution she will clean up her mess, ask her, "How will you do this? What will you be thinking as you work? Will you be thinking angry thoughts about me? Will you be thinking you are a bad person? Or will you be thinking that it's OK to make a mistake and you are a person who can fix things? You decide—it's your choice."

Your Turn

Think for a moment of a situation currently facing you where you might choose to shift your mind set. Here are some questions to help you.

1. What kind of person do I want to be in this difficult situation?

2. What do I want to take from this experience—a pearl or a hunk of dirt?

3. How can I view this as an opportunity to strengthen myself rather than as a punishment?

4. What will I do to be the person I want to be? How can I strengthen myself and gain self-balance? How can I make a self-restitution?

17. EVALUATE YOUR MESSAGE

GOALS

▶ To evaluate the impact of nonverbal messages

▶ To evaluate the impact of rhetorical questions

▶ To evaluate whether you practice Restitution both personally and professionally

▶ To understand the importance of incubation time in helping a student make a restitution plan

---

REFERENCE

▶ *Restitution,* pages 90-91, 108

HANDOUTS

▶ Fact and Opinion (page 101)

▶ Tone of Voice (page 102)

▶ It's Not What You Say, It's How You Say It (page 103)

FACILITATOR'S NOTES

▶ This section focuses on the messages we, as educators, convey to our students. Issues discussed are:

- Fact and Opinion
- Nonverbal Messages
- Rhetorical Questions

▶ When discussing a problem situation with students, it is very important that educators do not impose their subjective perceptions of the situation. A teacher involved with misbehaving students must focus on the facts of the situation—what was directly observed—rather than her interpretations. She must also help the students do the same. See the activity "Fact and Opinion" on page 101.

▶ Be aware of your nonverbal and tonal messages. Explain the importance of the tone of voice we use in helping students plan a restitution. Research on conversation has indicated that how you convey a message is more important than the specific words you use. Your vocal tone carries 35% of the message, your face and body carry 55%, and the words carry only 10%. The tone of voice is especially important in asking the following questions:

- "What do we believe in our classroom about how we treat each other?"

- "What do we believe in our classroom about replacing another's property?"

- "Are you the kind of person who treats others with respect?"

- "Are you the kind of person who can make restitution when you make a mistake?"

The most effective tone when asking these questions is direct and sincere—not controlling. These questions teach children that we are not searching for fault, we are searching for a remedy. We are interested in the kind of people they are becoming.

Model tone and body messages. Use the five different "Positions of Control" (Punisher, Guilter, Buddy, Monitor, Manager) to model different tones of voice and body language in asking the following question: "What kind of a person do you want to be?"

▶ Avoid rhetorical questions. When asking questions of misbehaving students it is easy to become rhetorical. A rhetorical question is a statement with a question at the end. The goal of the rhetorical question is for the listener to give the answer the questioner wants. The way the question is asked makes it difficult for the child to give a different answer. The student can only answer yes or no. Research indicates that people who are not in power positions tend to use rhetorical questions more frequently. These people are more inclined to mask the source of the decision. In helping students make restitution plans, it is important to avoid using rhetorical questions. Instead, ask open questions which allow students to share what they are thinking and doing (see questions in italics).

- You know what the rule is, don't you? *What's the rule?*

- You weren't where you were supposed to be, were you? *Where were you supposed to be?*

- You know you shouldn't have done that, right? *What did you do?*

- This is important to you, isn't it? *Is this getting you what you want? What do you want?*

- You want to do better, don't you? *Do you want to figure out a better way?*

When paraphrasing back to children, make factual statements rather than judgmental ones. For example, "I saw you put your hand on his shoulder." This stabilizes the success identity.

ACTIVITIES

▶ Fact and Opinion

This exercise is designed to assist participants in seeing the difference between observed behavior and one's interpretation of that behavior. The activity shows the participants that there can be many different interpretations of the same incident. It also helps them isolate and identify the observed behaviors that everyone can agree upon.

Pantomime

1. Ask two volunteers, a male and a female member of the group, to assist her in an activity.

2. Instruct the group to observe a pantomime and tell them to be aware of what they see.

3. The volunteers do their pantomime. Because of the ambiguity of the situation, a good scenario would be a man trying to attract a woman's attention.

Debriefing

1. After the activity, ask the group the question, "What happened?" Then, using a flip chart and pen, list about ten responses from the group, *leaving spaces between the responses*. It is important to write down anything they say, even if it is a flip comment or a joke.

2. The next step is to define for the group the difference between fact and opinion. A fact is something that we can all observe and agree upon. An opinion is our interpretation of that factual evidence—our perception.

3. Ask the group how many statements on the flip chart are fact. Generally, there may be one or two out of ten observations which the group can agree are observable facts. (E.g., "She left the room.") Often there are none.

4.. Discuss the concept that our opinions are based on facts. We don't form them in a vacuum. Then go over each opinion on the chart and ask, "What fact did you observe that supports this opinion?" (For example: *Opinion* – She doesn't like him; *Fact* – He leaned over twice and both times she turned her head away.)

5. Write these secondary observations (the facts which support the opinions) in the space left between the initial group responses. The group members can now see how opinions can be traced back to factual observations.

6. Discuss key words that tell us when an opinion is being expressed. They are words such as: seemed, appeared, thought, believe, felt, tried, wanted. Remember that the feeling component of our behavior is internal, therefore it really can't be an observable fact. Motivation also comes from within and therefore can't be directly observed. Tie these ideas to the Control Theory concept that we each create our own reality through our perceptions of the world.

Questionnaire: Review and Discussion

Divide participants into pairs and ask them to discuss the facts and opinions on the handout on the next page. Have them mark any statements on which they disagree and then discuss these with the entire group. There are several statements which are ambiguous or do not provide enough information (#6, #9, #15).

Note: In reviewing these statements, don't stress whether they are right or wrong. Instead, ask the group what needs to be added to each statement to make it a fact. What part of each statement is fact? What part of each statement is opinion?

Answers: (1) O; (2) F; (3) O; (4) O; (5) F; (6) A; (7) O; (8) F; (9) A; (10) O; (11) O; (12) F; (13) O; (14) O; (15) A.

▶ Tone of Voice ☆

Pass out the handout or use as a transparency "Tone of Voice" on page 102. Invite participants to practice the personal involvement points with a partner.

▶ It's Not What You Say, It's How You Say It ☆

Pass out the handout "It's Not What You Say, It's How You Say It" on page 103. Read and discuss the first page together. Invite participants to do the activity on the other pages.

▶ Crooked and Straight Questions ☆

In pairs, state a "crooked question" (rhetorical question) and then change it to a "straight question." Example:

- "You're going to give me a ride, aren't you?" *(crooked)*

- "Will you give me a ride?" *(straight)*

Fact and Opinion

Mark each of the statements as opinion (O), fact (F), or too ambiguous (A) to identify as either fact or opinion.

1. _____   He is agitating his fellow students.

2. _____   He was out of his seat three times this afternoon.

3. _____   He likes him.

4. _____   He is uncooperative.

5. _____   He hit him.

6. _____   He stood in the doorway when she tried to pass.

7. _____   He doesn't care.

8. _____   He didn't come to the meeting.

9. _____   She called on Joe three times and he did not answer.

10. _____   She is picking on him.

11. _____   He is disinterested.

12. _____   Twice he didn't answer.

13. _____   He is aggressive.

14. _____   He is manipulative.

15. _____   He has no money.

This exercise is from Doing It *by Diane Chelsom Gossen.*

Tone of Voice

What Carries the Message?

Words 10%

Tone 35%

Nonverbal 55%

Personal Involvement

1. Use a calm voice.

2. Lean forward (belonging) or back (freedom), depending on the need of the student.

3. Make eye contact. Don't force this with a student who is withdrawn.

4. Sit at the same level as the student.

5. Keep posture open. Don't cross your arms.

6. Repeat some version of "We need to work it out."

7. Listen and affirm.

8. Try to understand and recognize the child's point of view.

Sometimes when we use questions to frame up a restitution we use a critical or guilting tone. Did you know that the words are only 10% of any message you deliver? How can this be? Research on conversation has indicated that *how* you convey a message is more important than the specific words you use. Your vocal tone carries 35% of the message, your face and body carry the other 55%. Think of the different manners in which you might convey the following messages:

- I don't care.
- It's up to you—whatever you say.
- Really.
- Is this helping?

Did you notice the same words can mean exactly the opposite depending on how you say them? Understanding how little of the message is conveyed by the words can help you when listening to a person reporting a conversation secondhand. It is natural for each of us to report our side of it in the most positive tone of voice possible. Thus, the person who did not observe or hear the interchange is sometimes confused. They can't understand why the other person "reacted" to such a reasonable approach! Yes, the words were reasonable ("Do you need my help?"), but the way they were expressed gave an entirely different message ("Do you need my help, stupid!").

Where do our nonverbal and tonal messages come from? They come from our ego states. The transactional-analysis model says we have three main ways of thinking about ourselves: the parent state, the adult state, and the child state. Depending upon how we are thinking, we change our tone and gestures. We are speaking in the parent ego state when we point our fingers at people. If we talk down to them, we are perceived as patronizing and they will probably resent it. We are speaking in the adult ego state when we use a reasonable, non-emotional tone. This is the mode in which to give information. Our child ego state has three parts. There is the rebellious child which comes out when someone approaches us in a critical parental manner. There is the fearful child which we can hear in our voices when we are upset. Then there is the free child which appears when we are having fun and being creative. This child is where much of our positive energy comes from.

ACTIVITY GUIDELINES

Think about what you have just read, now ask the following question, with three different ego states in mind.

- a pointing, critical parent
- a rebellious child
- an adult

The questions to ask are:

- *What do you want?*
- *What are you doing?*

In the Workplace

The best voice to use when doing any kind of business is the adult voice. This tone is for giving or getting information. This is the tone of an effective supervisor, a competent employee, or an objective board member. The following questions could be perceived to be offensive when asked in the wrong tone. Practice asking the following questions in a calm, non-judgmental voice.

- When can we expect this to be done?
- Where were you when we had the meeting on Tuesday?
- How much did you spend?

Now practice asking the questions in an accusing tone. Do you hear the difference? How does the person being spoken to feel? Does he/she want to cooperate with you?

18. RESTITUTION GUIDELINES

GOAL

▶ To be able to summarize the important points of Restitution

REFERENCE

▶ *Restitution*, pages 107-129

HANDOUTS

▶ Guidelines for Helping a Student Get to Restitution (page 106)

▶ Getting to Restitution (pages 107-108)

FACILITATOR'S NOTES

▶ Allow incubation time.

Artists know that before they create, they need an incubation period during which the right brain can work on the challenge. To us, this incubation may be recognized as taking a walk when in conflict (leaving the problem alone only to find it solved on our return) or "just sleeping on it." It is not uncommon to wake up in the night with the answer clearly formed in one's mind. This is the holistic brain working on the gestalt. Each of us has a control system attempting to reduce error. Conflict is error. The brain will continue to work on conflict until it creates either an action or a perception shift that will resolve the dilemma. We experience a pleasure signal when this creation has been recognized. It may be expressed as a reflective gleam in your eyes or laughing out loud as the solution presents itself to you. This almost always occurs after a period of incubation. Teachers who often demand an answer immediately need to be aware of the importance of incubation time. Too often we ignore the random answers which seem irrelevant rather than mining them for the truths they present. When in extreme conflict, the brain works rapidly toward restitution, especially if survival is perceived to be threatened. However, in most situations, it is better for us to allow a time where ideas and solutions can be incubated.

▶ Don't frighten.

Current brain research also teaches us that when a person is frightened, their brain downshifts to focus on survival. It is extremely difficult to create solutions because the person can't think.

▶ Restitution can't be forced.

Not all students are ready for Restitution and the process cannot be forced. Restitution should be invited, but never demanded. The words "have to" make Restitution a consequence. If a student doesn't want to make a restitution, ask yourself these questions:

- Am I using a non-coercive tone of voice?
- Have I stabilized the student's identity?
- Have I validated the misbehavior?
- Have I identified the belief tied to the behavior?
- Have I said things like "I want to work things out"?

If you have used all these strategies and the student is still not interested in making a restitution, then issue a consequence. Say to the student: "If you don't want to fix it, I'll be in a position where I have to… [state consequence] I don't want to do that. I want to work it out."

ACTIVITIES

▶ Guidelines for Helping a Student Get to Restitution

Pass out the handouts or use as transparencies "Guidelines for Helping a Student Get to Restitution" (page 106) and "Getting to Restitution" (pages 107-108). Discuss as a group.

1. As soon as possible, say, "It's OK to make a mistake. The most important thing is to fix it."

2. If the student is caught in guilt, ask, "Are you being a good friend to yourself in this situation? Is that what a good friend would say?" Ask the student to evaluate their self-talk.

3. Ask the student if they are behaving like the kind of person they want to be? When helpful, tie this question to the beliefs of the class or family. (Be sure to monitor your tone of voice so it doesn't sound like preaching.)

4. Invite students to make amends or a restitution to their self-picture.

5. Make a plan.

6. Ask the students to evaluate their own perspective (reactive versus proactive). "What are you thinking about this situation? What are you saying to yourself? Is it helping you?"

1. Say as soon as possible, "It's OK to make a mistake. The main thing is to fix it. I'm not looking for fault." Students can then focus on solutions to the problem rather than how they will defend themselves.

2. If a student is focused on guilt ask, "Are you being a good friend to yourself?" Help the person understand that negative self-talk is using up energy needed for problem-solving.

3. Say, "You didn't do that for no reason. There is something you needed." Have the person identify the need she was attempting to meet or protect by her behavior.

4. Ask, "Could you have done worse?" Identify an even less effective behavior that the person could have chosen.

RESTITUTION...

- takes practice.
- is not easy.
- takes time and patience.
- is invited, not forced.
- is tied to common beliefs which we develop with the group.
- depends on belief in the concept of self-evaluation and self-discipline.
- asks that you separate yourself from the situation emotionally.
- emphasizes the direction you're going, not where you've been.
- models making mistakes and fixing them.
- strengthens everyone involved.

WHAT CAN I CHANGE? (3 THINGS)

1. My picture

2. My behavior

3. My perception (level)

Each of these can be evaluated and modified.

- All behavior is purposeful; even behavior we don't like.

- Every "bad" behavior is an attempt to avoid something worse.

- Don't ask a person to give up a behavior until you understand what need it has been meeting.

SELF-EVALUATION*

- What do you want?

- What are you prepared to do to get what you want?

- What question do you want to have answered when you leave?

- Is there any change in your thinking about the need to reach your goals? If so, what is it?

- If you aren't getting what you want, what are you doing right now in an attempt to get it? Self-evaluate.

- Who can help you? How will you get this help?

- If you are feeling discouraged, what are you doing to help yourself feel hopeful? What else can you do? Self-evaluate.

WHAT TO DO WHEN YOU ARE CRITICIZED

- Recognize that the person is trying to keep you focused on the feeling component of your behavior. If they succeed, you'll be off balance!

- Think! Keep yourself in balance by saying to yourself, "Isn't it interesting how this person is trying to control me? Will I let it work on me?"

- Act! Ask the person what they want. This question keeps you in control of yourself. When people criticize, say, "You're telling me what you don't want. Instead, tell me how you would like to see this solved."

- Stick up for yourself. If you don't agree with the person, say, "I understand that is your opinion; I see it a little differently."

- Don't criticize them. If you do this, you become part of the problem instead of part of the solution.

WHAT TO DO WHEN YOU'RE ATTACKED

- Say, "This is not how you get what you want from me."

- Say, "This conversation is not helping. I don't want to fight with you."

- Say, "I'll talk to you when you calm down. I want to work this out later," and then leave.

Developed from questions given to me by Jeanette McDaniels

Afterword

From the Second Edition of Restitution

> "There is no adequate defense, except stupidity, against the impact of a new idea."
>
> — *Percy W. Bridgman*

AFTERWORD

For the past two years, I have been working with school systems throughout the U.S. and Canada to help them implement the ideas in this book. These experiences have confirmed what I already knew: *teaching and implementing restitution is not easy.*

With the learning of any new theory, there is plenty of room for misinterpretation or misunderstanding. Learning about the Restitution Model and the theory behind it is no exception. I will therefore address some of the concerns and problems that educators have encountered as they begin to use this model.

In order to implement Restitution, it is very important that you understand the theory behind it, Control Theory. The problem is that many of society's assumptions are contrary to this theory. The following beliefs, which are rooted in stimulus-response theory, have been the foundations of twentieth-century education:

- We are externally motivated.
- We are controlled by others' behaviors.
- We all share a single reality.
- Positive reinforcement is desirable.
- Mistakes are bad and to be avoided.
- The way to change "bad" behaviors in others is by causing them discomfort through guilt or criticism.

Control Theory refutes these beliefs. To attempt implementing Restitution without understanding Control Theory is to risk the misinterpretations that are inherent in the stimulus-response view of life. Control Theory states that:

- We are internally motivated.

- We can only control ourselves, not others. Others can try to control us with superior force, but ultimately we decide if it's going to change what we believe.

- Each of us has a separate reality. We all perceive the same situation with different eyes.

- Positive reinforcement is coercive and hinders people from meeting their need for freedom.

- Making mistakes is the best way to learn. Inaction due to fear of mistakes closes down the reorganization system that we use to find creative solutions.

- All behavior is purposeful and "misbehavior" is chosen to avoid a worse option. Criticism and guilt are not effective ways to change someone's behavior—they only engender negative self-esteem.

I would like to discuss some further difficulties that educators have encountered as they integrate Restitution into their schools.

Some schools become so enthused about implementing Restitution that they completely abandon their previous framework for discipline—eliminating all rules and consequences. Most children (as well as adults) are not able to change direction so quickly. Students begin to test their limits and, because these limits have been abandoned, teachers find themselves trying to persuade children to behave (therefore reverting to a coercive behavior). *I do not advocate giving up rules and consequences.* These limits must be kept in place to fall back on for those children not ready to practice self-discipline.

Another misinterpretation has been to focus on reparation to the victim, rather than self-reparation by the offender. If we over-emphasize retribution to the victims and ignore the crucial second half of the restitution—the offender taking responsibility for strengthening and healing himself—the restitution is ineffective. If the restitution is dependent on the victim's acceptance, the offender may be denied an opportunity to strengthen himself. Keep the focus on self-restitution by helping the student separate the proposed restitution from the victim's acceptance.

Working on beliefs at the classroom level is essential to maintaining a sound base for restitution. The main question in framing a restitution is "What do we believe?" If the students and teachers have not already discussed this and formed a group social contract, the beliefs that individual children hold may not be aligned with those of the school. If this is the case, begin working with students to develop common principles such as cooperation, a respect for others and their property, a value on quality work, and appreciation of the uniqueness of the individual.

Several teachers have told me that they are often involved with a dozen students with individual restitution plans underway at once. The teacher's main job is to teach the class. Doing this much individual counseling with students takes an inordinate amount of time and energy away from achieving this primary goal. Remember that two or three plans at a time are enough. Once you begin to over-invest yourself, chances are that you may be more tempted to give up on Restitution. Keep in mind that this shift in thinking and doing takes time and patience. The plans themselves are not the most important aspect to Restitution. Building strength results from a thoughtful and consistent follow-through on the plans, self-evaluation, and replanning by the students. Go slowly. Practice making plans for restitution with your whole class. Less time will then be needed for individual cases. These opportunities also provide students with some practical and guided experience with making restitution.

A common problem is forced restitution. A mandatory restitution is always a false restitution. If a student is required to make a restitution, the act is only a consequence— void of any personal growth for either the offender or the victim. Restitution is invited, not demanded. In most cases, if a child does not want to make restitution, the teacher should use a consequence until the child is ready to practice self-discipline.

Be aware if students haven't learned restitution and we ask them, "What can you do to fix it?" Most of the time their suggestions are consequences which may be demeaning or weakening to them. They don't understand it should be a healing, strengthening reparation. When this happens we have to ask the child, "How will this get you stronger?" We may even need to say, "If it isn't getting you stronger, it isn't restitution." This is a crucial point because if the child is being strengthened through each discipline encounter, only if this happens will there be a reduction in discipline problems.

The focus of Restitution must always be on assisting students in strengthening themselves. To discomfort your students is to control them. Coercive behaviors do not teach them self-discipline. We all make mistakes. When we do, we are simply not being the people we want to be. In the face of a mistake, if we can create a successful restitution, we strengthen ourselves by becoming the people we are capable of being. Not only do we, as individuals, benefit greatly from this process, but so does society as a whole.

Appendix

Notes to the Facilitator

"To teach is to learn twice over."

— *Joseph Joubert*

LEAD MANAGERS

Restitution is a process. It takes time to shift our mental model of discipline from a stimulus-response approach to a Control Theory approach. Modeling lead-management helps teachers make this paradigm shift and implement Restitution.

Practice the "loose-tight" connection—"tight" on the beliefs about people and "loose" on the implementation of Restitution.

As a lead-manager who is implementing Restitution, it is important to live and work by the beliefs of Control Theory.

- *Lead managers take risks and learn from their mistakes.*
  It's OK to make a mistake. Encourage teachers to experiment and take risks in implementing Restitution.

- *Lead managers help teachers maintain a success identity.*
  Teachers will be internally motivated to move forward.

- *Lead managers influence others.*
  Instead of mandating Restitution, influence teachers to use lead-management techniques and implement Restitution concepts. Remember that you can't control others.

- *Lead managers try to understand other teachers' pictures.*

Remember that everybody has their own unique picture of discipline.

Provide teachers with a variety of resources, materials, experiences, and opportunities to learn more about Control Theory and Restitution. Lead managers are learners. Lead managers do not impose a timetable on others. Realize that teachers change beliefs slowly as a result of gaining new information and experiences.

MODELING LESS COERCIVE MANAGEMENT

It is essential that workshop leaders seek opportunities to model less coercive management in their own personal styles as well as to reveal these strategies in the group process. In every group there will be moments when the leader is tempted to coerce the group simply because of the dynamics of the situation. Not only is this normal, but it also provides a learning opportunity as the leader reveals her intent, examines how the group senses it, and then discusses better and worse possible options with the group. Below are some guidelines for modeling less coercive management in your workshops.

1. *Welcome The Opportunity:* When establishing the logistics of the workshop, participants will almost always ask for changes or exceptions. As the workshop leader, welcome these requests as opportunities to model less coercive management.

2. *Seating Choices:* "Familiarity Breeds Contentment" – In groups, most people sit with their friends because it is comfortable. On the other hand, in one of my workshops a participant chose to sit by himself apart from the group, even though the course was structured around interactive exercises. What does a leader do? Does it really matter who sits where? Are you going to impose your will? What would *you* do?

3. *Size of Groups:* "Plus or Minus" – When doing small group activities, no matter what size the leader asks for, there are always those who wish to add in one or more extra persons to their group because of their own particular belonging needs. What would you do?

4. *Lunch Hour:* "Eat to Live or Live to Eat" – Unless the group is accustomed to Boss-Management there will often be questions about the time and length of lunch hour and people will have different preferences. The same may be true for starting and ending times if they are negotiable. How would you deal with these issues?

5. *Working Inside or Outside:* "Please May We" – If the opportunity arises, there is frequently a request to work outside in warm weather, especially in northern climates. What would you do?

6. *Dress:* Where there is a dress code, a request is often made for more casual wear. What would you do? Whatever the request, the leader should, if possible, practice "Yes Management." In order to be a "yes manager," the leader must know her own needs and be aware of the needs of the organizing agency. A leader must be able to meet her needs, do her job, and not over-expend energy on setting the conditions or the learners will suffer.

RESISTANT GROUPS

Sometimes people question the structure of the group as a challenge to the leader. They want to see if the leader is going to coerce them. For example, a group of teachers who have regular work hours of 7:30 a.m. to 2:30 p.m. might attend a workshop scheduled from 8:00 a.m. to 3:30 p.m. If they ask what time the workshop ends (in the hopes of changing this time), I ask, "What were you told that the workshop hours would be?" If there is silence, I provide them with information. If the group shares with me that they usually finish their day at 2:30, I focus on my role as workshop leader by using terms such as *policy, protocol,* and *expectation.* I might ask, "What is the district's expectation in regards to this workshop's ending time? What does your contract specify with regards to in-service workshops?" If they are vague about the expectations, I ask, "Are you interested in clarification? If so, who has the answers to these questions?"

If I need to give information to the group, I make a preliminary statement: "I want to give you some information about the hours I need to spend with you in order to meet the requirements of this program." I then give the information about the expectations on me as a trainer and provide choices: "How we schedule those hours is of no consequence to me as long as we put in all the necessary time. I can start earlier or end later. Are there any restricting parameters in the system or can we decide?" If they are not certain who has the power to make this decision, I ask, "How can we resolve this? Who can help us?" If pushed for a change in workshop times and I don't know the parameters, I say, "In this case, it's not my job to change the schedule without informing the person who hired me."

The goal of less coercive management is to achieve a "loose-tight" connection. We need to be tight on what we want to achieve and loose on how the goal is accomplished. This gives people choice and helps them assume responsibility. In conclusion to this issue I would say, "Personally, it makes no difference to me what specific hour the workshop ends. The decision is not mine alone to make. What matters to me is that you are open to examining the ideas I have to present. No specific time frame will make you more open to learn. Nor will it inhibit you unless you choose to let it be a barrier."

What I refuse to do is to try to force workshop participants to do anything. Instead, my job is to model what we believe. In our model we believe it is impossible for a person to control another person. A person in authority can only state what he will do if the person under supervision does not comply with the directive. If the person under supervision does not mind being discomforted, if freedom is more important, he will choose disobedience. Then the supervisor follows through with a consequence. Ideally, the strategies that we teach help us to avoid such an impasse.

Discuss some strategies that you have used when dealing with resistant groups. For example:

- The principal has forced the teachers to come to a workshop on discipline.

- Probation workers have been mandated by law to assist young offenders in developing options for making restitution.

- The superintendent has told principals that they will be evaluated on their lead-management skills. However, these principals do not know what this management style is and are attending your workshop to learn.

How would you deal with these situations? Could you use these opportunities to model your lead-management skills?

READINGS

Covey, Stephen R. *Principle-Centered Leadership*. New York: Simon and Schuster, 1991.

Glasser, William. *Control Theory: A New Explanation of How We Control Our Lives*. New York: HarperCollins, 1984.

———. *The Quality School: Managing Students Without Coercion*. New York: HarperCollins, 1990.

———. *The Quality School Teacher*. New York: HarperCollins, 1993.

———. *Reality Therapy*. New York: HarperCollins, 1969.

———. *Stations of the Mind*. New York: HarperCollins, 1981.

Good, E. Perry. *In Pursuit of Happiness*. Chapel Hill, NC: New View Publications, 1987.

———. *Helping Kids Help Themselves*. Chapel Hill, NC: New View Publications, 1992.

———. *Overall Direction*. Chapel Hill, NC: New View Publications, 1996.

Gossen, Diane Chelsom. *Helping Disruptive and Unresponsive Students*. Salt Lake City: The Video Journal of Education, 1992.

———. *My Child Is a Pleasure to Live With*. Saskatoon: Chelsom Consultants Limited, 1997.

———. *Restitution: Restructuring School Discipline*, Second Revised Edition. Chapel Hill, NC: New View Publications, 1996.

———. *Restitution For Teens*. Saskatoon: Chelsom Consultants Limited, 1997.

———. *Restitution Video Staff Development Program*. Saskatoon: Chelsom Consultants Limited, 1997.

Gossen, Diane Chelsom, and Judy Anderson. *Creating the Conditions: Leadership for Quality Schools*. Chapel Hill, NC: New View Publications, 1995.

Greene, Brad. *New Paradigms for Creating Quality Schools*. Chapel Hill, NC: New View Publications, 1995.

Kohn, Alfie. *Beyond Discipline*. Alexandria, VA: Association for Supervision and Curriculum Development, 1996.

———. *Punished By Rewards*. New York: Houghton Mifflin Company, 1993.

McFadden, Judy. *The Simple Way to Raise a Good Kid*. Sydney, Australia: Horowitz Grahame, PTY Ltd., 1988.

Powers, William T. *Behavior: The Control of Perception*. Chicago: Aldine Publishing Co., 1973.

Ross, Rupert. *Returning to the Teachings*. Toronto: Penguin Books, 1996.

Senge, Peter. *The Fifth Discipline*. New York: Doubleday, 1990.

Sullo, Robert A. *Teach Them To Be Happy,* Second Revised Edition. Chapel Hill, NC: New View Publications, 1993.

Wubbolding, Robert E. *Understanding Reality Therapy*. New York: HarperCollins, 1991.

———. *Using Reality Therapy*. New York: HarperCollins, 1988.

INDEX OF ACTIVITIES

☆ *"Inside-Out" Activities. See page 2 for explanation.*

INDEX OF HANDOUTS